GATHERED LIGHT

THE POETRY OF JONI MITCHELL'S SONGS

Edited by Lisa and John Sornberger

Published in 2013 by Sumach Press, an imprint of Three O'Clock Press Inc.
425 Adelaide St. W. #200 | Toronto ON | M5V3C1
www.threeoclockpress.com

Library and Archives Canada Cataloguing in Publication

Gathered light : the poetry of Joni Mitchell's songs / eds.,
Lisa and John Sornberger.

Essays.
ISBN 978-1-927513-12-5

1. Mitchell, Joni, 1943- --Criticism and interpretation.
2. Creative ability. I. Sornberger, Lisa II. Sornberger, John

ML420.M523G38 2013   782.42164092   C2013-901761-5

Also available as an e-book, ISBN 978-1-92751-314-9

Cover painting: © Joni Mitchell

Printed and bound in Canada by Marquis

GATHERED LIGHT

THE POETRY OF JONI MITCHELL'S SONGS

Edited by Lisa and John Sornberger

TABLE OF CONTENTS

URGE FOR GOING	1	COURT AND SPARK	125
MARCIE	5	HELP ME	128
SONG TO A SEAGULL	10	FREE MAN IN PARIS	132
CACTUS TREE	17	TROUBLE CHILD	136
I DON'T KNOW WHERE I STAND	23	SHADOWS AND LIGHT	140
THE FIDDLE AND THE DRUM	25	COYOTE	145
BOTH SIDES NOW	30	FURRY SINGS THE BLUES	150
FOR FREE	34	HEJIRA	154
LADIES OF THE CANYON	37	SONG FOR SHARON	158
BIG YELLOW TAXI	41	SISTOWBELL LANE	163
WOODSTOCK	45	BLACK CROW	167
THE CIRCLE GAME	52	DREAMLAND	173
ALL I WANT	59	THE SILKY VEILS OF ARDOR	177
CAREY	65	GOD MUST BE A BOOGIE MAN	180
BLUE	72	THE WOLF THAT LIVES IN LINDSEY	183
CALIFORNIA	75	CHINESE CAFÉ/UNCHAINED MELODY	188
RIVER	84	LAKOTA	193
A CASE OF YOU	92	CHEROKEE LOUISE	200
THE LAST TIME I SAW RICHARD	101	SEX KILLS	208
BANQUET	105	THE MAGDALENE LAUNDRIES	211
FOR THE ROSES	110	SHINE	221
JUDGEMENT OF THE MOON AND STARS	117		

"URGE FOR GOING" AND THE LUMINOSITY OF GENIUS—NATHAN WISE 3
NOTES ON "MARCIE" FATA MORGANA & HERE AND NOW—ALISON MEYERS 7
SONG TO A SEAGULL—DARYL PERCH 12
RECONNECTING OURSELVES WITH NATURE—ROSIE GALLANT 16
"LIKE A CACTUS TREE": COMING OF AGE WITH JONI MITCHELL'S MUSIC—RICHARD FLYNN 19
I DON'T KNOW WHERE I STAND—JUNE BISANTZ 24
THE FIDDLE AND THE DRUM—NATHAN WISE 27
BOTH SIDES NOW—FELICITY HARLEY 32
PASSED BY/FOR FREE—WINKY GORDON 36
TRINA WEARS HER WAMPUM BEADS—TRINA ROBBINS 39
BIG YELLOW TAXI, OR THE DEMISE OF THE NATURAL WORLD—RAVI SHANKAR 43
STARDUST IN THE GARDEN: ON THE OPPOSITIONAL POETRY OF "WOODSTOCK"—JON ANDERSEN 47
I AM STARDUST—SUSAN DEER CLOUD 49
ROUND AND ROUND—KRISTIN ROUND GROVES 54
UP AND DOWN—JOHN SORNBERGER 56
ALL I WANT—ALEXANDER MACK 61
ALL I WANT—KATHLEEN McELROY 63
THE CREE WANDERER & FOR JONI—LOUISE B. HALFE (SKY DANCER) 67
CAREY—MAUREEN CROTEAU 70
INSPIRED BY THE SONG "BLUE"—RANDY JOHNSON 73
CALIFORNIA: AGAINST AUTOBIOGRAPHY—EDMOND CHIBEAU 77
"YOUR LIFE BECOMES A TRAVELOGUE" WITH JONI MITCHELL—PATTI PARLETTE 79
JOURNALING "THE RIVER" (A FICTIONAL WORK)—WILLA CORRENTI 86
RIVER—JILL ROBINSON 91
CAFETERIA (A CASE OF YOU)—MICHAEL CORRENTI 94
BE PREPARED TO BLEED—BRENT CALDERWOOD 97
THE LAST TIME I SAW RICHARD—KIM ADDONIZIO 103
WINTER 1972—ANJANI THOMAS 107
THREE POEMS INSPIRED BY "FOR THE ROSES"—LYN LIFSHIN 113
CONFLUENCE—LISA SORNBERGER 119
THE PORTAL AND THE LANGUAGE—STEVEN ALBAHARI 127
THE BEGUINE—COLEEN J. McELROY 130
SPEAKING WITH DAVID GEFFEN REGARDING "FREE MAN IN PARIS"—LISA SORNBERGER 134
TROUBLE CHILD—STEVE STARGER 138
LIGHT AND SHADOWS—PATRICIA SMITH 142
COYOTE—TERESE KARMEL 148
JONI, YOU'RE A RICH MAN, TOO—CORNELIUS EADY 152
HEJIRA—SO MUCH COULD NOT BE EXPRESSED—BESSY REYNA 156
JONI—SHARON BELL VEER 161
THE CANDLE IN THE WINDOW—SUE/SIOUX TABBAT WURZEL 165
BLACK CROW, BARE TREE—PIT PINEGAR 169
DREAMLAND—BARBARA LaFLESH 175
FOR JONI—AMY BYINGTON 179
THE PLAN IS IN THE DOORWAY—FOR JONI MITCHELL AND IN MEMORY OF CHARLES MINGUS—FRED WAH 181
ON "THE WOLF THAT LIVES IN LINDSEY"—PAUL LISICKY 185
WEREWOLVES OF LOS ANGELES—SEAN MURPHY 186
A THREAD OF JONI—JILL BULLOCK McALLISTER 190
CHINESE CAFÉ/UNCHAINED MELODY—LARRY KLEIN 191
THIS AINT NO KUMBAYAH!—JAMISON MAHTO 196
CREE MARY IS MY REAL NAME—BETH CUTHAND 202
ABOUT TWO GIRLS—PATRICIA WILSON 204
CHEROKEE LOUISE—JOHN C. SANDERS 206
TIDES—PETER KOUZMOV 210
SHAME ILLUMINATED: AN EXPLORATION OF "THE MAGDALENE LAUNDIRES"—BROOKE ELISE AXTELL 213
"THE MAGDALENE LAUNDRIES" AND ME—WALLY LAMB 215
SHINE—PAMELA PEGG RUNKLE 223

The canoe passed shores crammed with trees, trees overhanging stony beaches, trees held back by rocky cliffs, pointed fir trees climbing its dark masses up the mountain sides, moonlight silvering their blackness.

Our going was imperceptible, the woman's steering paddle the only thing that moved, its silent cuts stirring phosphorus like white fire.

Time and texture faded, ceased to exist—day was gone, yet it was not night. Water was not wet or deep, just smoothness spread with light.

—From "Canoe" by Emily Carr

FOREWORD

LISA AND JOHN SORNBERGER

When great poets go within to find insight and inspiration, they often head straight into the shadows.

They become shadow lifters and the words they find to describe what they have discovered are like gathered light.

When we read or hear some of Joni Mitchell's poems, her words shine out to us in ways that remind us that we are "alive alive (and make us) want to get up and jive."

Other poems illuminate our own hardscrabble areas, and in ways that nourish deeper insight and inspire us.

The wisdom, art and impact of such poetry should be honored, and fifty-five contributors do so in this book.

This collection is reflective of the experience of innumerable others who have also been deeply affected by the poetry of Joni Mitchell.

Joni, paraphrasing Nietzsche, has said "There is a new kind of poet, a penitent of spirit... who writes in his own blood." Clearly, Joni Mitchell is that kind of poet.

Her poetry is genuine and genius. May the light shine on her, and her creative powers, always.

URGE FOR GOING

I awoke today and found
The frost perched on the town
It hovered in a frozen sky
Then it gobbled summer down
When the sun turns traitor cold
And all the trees are shivering in a naked row...
I get the urge for going
But I never seem to go

I get the urge for going
When the meadow grass is turning brown
And summertime is falling down and winter is closing in

I had a man in summertime
He had summer-colored skin
And not another girl in town
My darling's heart could win
But when the leaves fell on the ground
And bully winds came around
And pushed them face down in the snow...
He got the urge for going
And I had to let him go

He got the urge for going
When the meadow grass was turning brown
And summertime was falling down and winter was closing in

Now the warriors of winter give a cold triumphant shout
And all that stays is dying—all that lives is gettin' out
See the geese in chevron flight—
Flapping and racing on before the snow...
They've got the urge for going
And they've got the wings to go
They get the urge for going
When the meadow grass is turning brown
And summertime is falling down and winter is closing in

I'll ply the fire with kindling now
I'll pull the blankets up to my chin
I'll lock the vagrant winter out
And I'll bolt my wandering in
I'd like to call back summertime
And have her stay for just another month or so...
But she's got the urge for going
So I guess she'll have to go

She gets the urge for going
When the meadow grass is turning brown
And all her empire's falling down
And winter's closing in

And I get the urge for going
When the meadow grass is turning brown
And summertime is
Falling
Down

"URGE FOR GOING" AND THE LUMINOSITY OF GENIUS

NATHAN WISE

Her incomparable legacy has been firmly assured for more than a generation now: Joni Mitchell is the compleat artist—poet and storyteller of the first order, musician and painter—whose ability to affect the way we experience the natural world is undeniable. Consider, for example, this depiction in "Chelsea Morning": "And the sun poured in like butterscotch and stuck to all my senses." This brilliant simile has the power to forever alter the very way in which we perceive the morning sun as it illuminates a room, with a palpable, sensory image in an elegant description. This can be compared to the vibrant portrayal of sunlit wheat fields by Van Gogh (so evocative of motion and rhythm) and the resulting way in which we've never seen the landscape of southern France quite the same once we saw it through Van Gogh's eyes. Such is the proof of genius, in both instances, and our culture is all the richer for each.

In turn, there is in poetry no truer depiction of a moment in nature—the turning of a season, in this case—than Joni Mitchell's "Urge For Going." The magnificent North American landscape has been a beautiful setting for such luminaries as Longfellow and Whittier, Emerson and Whitman. Robert Frost's "Whose woods are these I think I know" introduced us to one of the most beloved snowscapes in poetry; and the Yukon winds that shriek through Robert Service's blustery quatrains make us search for the closest tavern with a red-hot potbellied stove to warm us and men gathered 'round it, telling tales. It is possible, however, that Mitchell may have been more immediately influenced by the work of fellow Canadian Ian Tyson, whose "Four Strong Winds" was already enormously popular when Mitchell arrived on the scene. Tyson's male protagonist thinks he'll "go out to Alberta, weather's good there in the fall" and entreats his reluctant sweetheart to join him; "But by then it would be winter, not too much for you to do / And the winds sure blow cold way out there." His tone seems hopeless, further emphasized by a persistent refrain ("Four strong winds that blow lonely") that dismisses her far too casually (almost misogynistically), as being as harsh as the weather, when he concludes that "our good times are all gone, and I'm bound for movin' on / I'll look for you if I'm ever back this way." (Notice that he says "if".)

Tyson also told a moving tale in "Someday Soon," in which a woman whose father disapproves of her rodeo-riding sweetheart still longs to follow him south to the U.S. ("Someday soon, going with him, someday soon"). This separation of lovers, and an undeniable sense of loneliness, are tangible themes in Tyson's work, and together with Canadian settings, Mitchell is perfectly poised for her own tale of lost love and faded summertime. It's almost as if she's offering the female perspective to "Four Strong Winds."

What makes Mitchell special, though, is the heartbreak that she injects into her portrayal of autumnal loss ("Falling Down") and winter bitterness, as she gives voice to every feature of the transition through personification of the recognizable elements. It's familiar because we have all experienced that first frost that crystallizes the brown grass and steals the warmth of the sun and the color from the sky. Mitchell casts the cold as a hovering, ravenous bird of prey that leaps from the page before us with threatening audacity, then devours all that was good and sweet and romantic of the summer. The theme of wanting to hold onto that sunnier, happier season is one that resonates throughout literature, but the striking thing about Mitchell's first frost is the anguish of expectation as the cold seems to wait for its perfect moment of greatest vulnerability ("shivering" and "naked") to pounce and feed, as if upon a feast. All of nature, in fact, seems to have turned against the lonely (and, later, abandoned) poet, even the "traitor" sun, which had been the embodiment of the heat of summer just yesterday. The "closing in" of the winter gives a claustrophobic effect to the threat of an enemy surrounding the town and suffocating the life out of everyone and everything.

Using "sense-memory" the way a great acting teacher elicits a genuine, precise emotion from an actor, Mitchell subjects the fragile, trembling, falling leaves to "bully winds" that push them "face down in the snow" in a mean, harsh act that isn't merely the natural order of things, but hard and unyieldingly cruel. It's the way that the class bully doesn't just tug the pigtails of the girl sitting in front of him, but pulls her down to the floor by that pigtail and holds her there and doesn't let her up. Thus the word "bully," though simple, disturbs and frightens because of Mitchell's masterful context.

Then, too, in addition to her sorrow that her man (he of the "summer-colored skin") has slipped away ("And I had to let him go"), as if she'd been transfixed and incapable of following (with her fear that "all that stays is dying"), the forsaken lover diligently stokes her fire for warmth. Poetically, the assonance of "ply" and "fire" is one of Mitchell's most beautiful. The long "I" sound is picked up repeatedly in "I" and "fly" and "summertime" (and maybe a subliminal "bye," as in farewell), which extends to her desire to "call back summertime / And have her stay for just another month or so," which in versification seduces us with its Shakespearian pentameter. I am also reminded of Leslie Bricusse's glorious contribution to Henry Mancini's haunting "Two For The Road": "In summertime the sun will shine / In winter we'll drink summer wine." That wine is a way to hold onto the warmth of the summer sun, as surely as Mitchell's solitary survivor uses the warmth of the fire to keep the winter out, to recall the love she knew in summer. Yet there a feeling of her own strength in resisting the urge for going that she herself has expressed ("but I never seem to go") and which she now bolts in, as summer, now an "empire," finally succumbs.

The storytelling, and the heartbreak intrinsic to the common themes of so much of the greatest art, elevates Mitchell in our eyes in the same fashion as "The Ballad of the Harp-Weaver" enshrines Edna St. Vincent Millay. Mitchell's protagonist, though left alone and solitary at last, still appears strong and self-sufficient, strangely fortified—as if by choice—and at the peak of her creative powers to define her position. The lyrical, narrative treasures yet to come—"That Song About The Midway," "For Free," "California," "Rainy Night House"—will be as transcendent to us, as if we were Dante's weary traveler emerging from the Inferno and glimpsing the stars above.

MARCIE

Marcie in a coat of flowers
Steps inside a candy store
Reds are sweet and greens are sour
Still no letter at her door
So she'll wash her flower curtains
Hang them in the wind to dry
Dust her tables with his shirt and
Wave another day goodbye

Marcie's faucet needs a plumber
Marcie's sorrow needs a man
Red is autumn—green is summer
Greens are turning and the sand
All along the ocean beaches
Stares up empty at the sky
Marcie buys a bag of peaches
Stops a postman passing by
And summer goes
Falls to the sidewalk like string and brown paper
Winter blows
Up from the river there's no one to take her
To the sea

Marcie dresses warm—its snowing
She takes a yellow cab uptown
Red is stop and green's for going
She sees a show—she rides back down
Down along the Hudson River
Past the shipyards in the cold
Still no letter's been delivered
Still the winter days unfold
Like magazines

Fading in dusty grey attics and cellars
Make a dream
Dream back to summer and hear how
He tells her
"Wait for me!"

Marcie leaves and doesn't tell us
Where or why she moved away
Red is angry—green is jealous
That was all she had to say
Someone thought they saw her Sunday
Window shopping in the rain
Someone heard she bought a one-way ticket
And went west again

NOTES ON "MARCIE"
FATA MORGANA

ALISON MEYERS

"I used to think my body was a container for love."

—Tracy K. Smith, "They May Love All That He Has Chosen and Hate All That He Has Rejected," *Life on Mars*

In her essay "Dickens in Eden" (*The New Yorker,* August 29, 2011), Jill Lepore writes, "Everyone in Dickens is either a jailer or a prisoner, and some, like Dickens himself, are both: the author, his own turnkey." Life as binary—red or green, sweet or sour, stop or go, anger or jealousy. Yet in Joni Mitchell's "Marcie," as in a Dickens novel, there is also the possibility of psychological liberation: a yellow cab drives through the lyrics, and twice something blooms or has blossomed in multiple colors—"coat of flowers" and "flower curtains." Defying simple geometry, parallel lines promise to connect in a circle of comprehension, or soar like sprung arrows into the changeable sky, along ocean beaches and shipyards, into shops and places of human agency and exchange. Marcie's tale of sorrow mirrors the story of many middle-class young women living in the United States in 1968. It was mine in 1970, caught between a fairy tale—waiting to be completed by romantic love— and forging a key to unlock the possible. "Marcie" stormed through my limited nineteen-year-old experience and for three more decades intermittently overtook me, the color of sadness dominating my days and nights. A letter at the door would bring perpetual summer, I persisted in thinking as, over and over, I swung between the adrenaline of pursuing unending, all-consuming love and the inevitable, deep well of disappointment.

Now that I'm re-considering "Marcie" as the Joni Mitchell song that still most compels me, for the first time I notice the obvious—that it's written in third person, an "us." Someone—a chorus of someones—is observing Marcie's obsession and choices, not without sympathy, but decidedly from a middle distance. The elders seem to know that her journey is just beginning, even if Marcie herself supposes she can't live without one particular man's single-minded devotion. What is the difference between *being* Marcie and *seeing* Marcie? For me, forty-plus years, pharmaceuticals and the occasional ability to step outside the picture. I somehow believe that Marcie, too, has survived her youth and that wherever she lives on the map, west or east, is telling her story in the first person and digging into complicated life.

HERE AND NOW

I.
Chatanooga, 1942

All his South here in memory's insistence. An afternoon
of dusty play, then an hour to breathe under grandmother's
ancient arbor, leafed shade through which hot minutes blink,
sudden sparks flashing on cool surfaces of streams.

Here it is baked earth where a boy daydreams
and a woman sings, notes holding motionless in etiolated
air, cupped palms bringing precious water to shore:
Sweet chariot, coming for to carry me home.

Dreamy child, you are sixty-seven, now remembering
or imagining, no longer able to believe in suffering
that finds a place to rest—not there, then, or here now
in this unremarkable greasy spoon north of Broadway,
red table beneath your fingers articulate with unnamed desire.

II.
Daily News

I will be your last good thing
because you are ever filled with want
and I, like you, helplessly desire
what never can remain for long.

Today they dig the last of the dead
from beneath the ruined weight
of earthquaked Golcuk. The stench
of murdered distant countries lingers
on our fingertips with the morning's
newsprint, mad sex of our times.

Soon enough we will join some
other ancient corpses we read about,
hundreds upon hundreds in tidy rows,
the marvel of refusing to rot into soft
desert earth a sanctification. Intricate
gilt, pungent linen, generations

of anonymous worn hands that wound
the magic cloth just so. While we can know
and feel and remember,
I will be your last good thing.

III.
Envoi

There is no heaven, we insisted, so tell me
where do I find you in the here and now?

A murder of crows wings from dark trees
by the roadside. Violent surge, observable strife
for open air, not solitary but together and at once.

Might never feel this way again,
Phoebe Snow proclaims from the car radio, as if
to say what is first or last is, in any case, unrepeatable.

The birds rise, a woman sings,
I watch and listen.

SONG TO A SEAGULL

Fly silly seabird
No dreams can possess you
No voices can blame you for sun on your wings
My gentle relations
Have names they must call me
For loving the freedom of all flying things
My dreams with the seagulls fly
Out of reach out of cry

I came to the city
And lived like old Crusoe
On an island of noise—in a cobblestone sea
And the beaches were concrete
And the stars paid a light bill
And the blossoms hung false on their store window trees
My dreams with the seagulls fly
Out of reach out of cry

Out of the city
And down to the seaside
To sun on my shoulders and wind in my hair
But sandcastles crumble
And hunger is human
And humans are hungry for worlds they can't share
My dreams with the seagulls fly
Out of reach out of cry

I call to a seagull
Who dives to the waters
And catches his silver-fine dinner
Alone
Crying where are the footprints
That danced on these beaches
And the hands that cast wishes
That sunk
Like a stone
My dreams with the seagulls fly
Out of reach out of cry

SONG TO A SEAGULL

DARYL PERCH

I chose to write about "Song To A Seagull" for its combination of evocative language and haunting chords. Joni Mitchell's poetry can stand alone, and her music sets the tone for her message while her distinctive, flute-like voice imprints it on the listener's soul.

"Song To A Seagull" is early Joni. It was written in 1968, the title track of her first album, produced when she was twenty-four. She and I were born the same year. Trust me, she was a lot more self-assured and accomplished than I was at that age.

While I was still figuring out who I wanted to be, she was already "the rage," as one critic put it, for her hit songs that had been covered by Judy Collins, Buffy Sainte-Marie and others. "Song To A Seagull" would be her first solo recording venture. Not only did she write the songs and perform vocals, guitar and piano on the album, she also painted the cover: a sunny montage of images evocative of the psychedelic posters of Peter Max.

At the time she wrote the title song, she was living in New York, lured by the burgeoning folk scene. I was there too, frequenting the womb-like cellars of Greenwich Village coffeehouses for the thrill of being entertained by hat-passing bards and future icons.

While my peers were discovering the freedom of legally ordering beer, I thirsted for mediocre coffee that came with a cover charge and the chance to feel on the cusp of hipness. Those aspiring artists who dropped by the Gaslight Cafe on MacDougal Street to play a set, read a poem or jam with their friends made me feel part of something big that we all sensed was happening.

Folk music heralded a cosmic cultural shift. Changes were speeding toward us and they were our generation's to seize.

Until my folk awakening, my musical exposure had been limited to a chair in the viola section of the high school orchestra and to my parents' big-band records. Those 78 RPM platters pumped out feel-good tunes designed to lift the spirits of post-war America. Early rock 'n roll was no more sophisticated.

What I discovered in the crowded New York coffeehouses was a stripped-down, acoustic sound in which the words were more important than the melody. These were serious lyrics—protest songs and minor-key laments that stirred my social conscience. To me they were calls to action.

Stop the war. Save the environment. Mistrust politicians. Question authority. Make a difference. I was hooked. I taught myself to play the guitar. I sensed in the lyrics of the era a promised freedom from the rigid social rules that had shaped my upbringing. Well-chosen words of those talented troubadours inspired me to believe that my destiny was open-ended. I would not be beholden to the expectations of women who went before me. I would not view an education as merely a hedge against early widowhood. Nor would I think of marriage or motherhood as a duty rather than an option.

Young women like me dared to dream of breaking free from the mores of our parents' time. Joni Mitchell, Joan Baez, Judy Collins and their contemporaries were our scouts. Their voices emboldened us to sing out and speak up. Suddenly, we had choices and our own unique music to make them by.

At twenty-four, Joni Mitchell had already mastered the art of weaving an evocative tapestry of images with a few strummed chords and a poetic ear. I was awed by her musical talent, of course, but also by her independence and insight, which I did not possess at that point in my life.

I was told that I could achieve anything if I worked hard for it and could overcome any obstacle before me as long as I followed the rules. She understood that life was more complicated and that rules often got in the way.

At the time she wrote "Song To A Seagull," Joni's creative urges were so strong that they compelled her to follow her muse. As a new mother, I had shifted my focus away from my own dreams and put them, along with my guitar, on the shelf.

Words, however, would remain my passion. They became my profession. As a journalist, I aspired to paint pictures with my pen. I used words to persuade and inform. As an editor, I saw the music in the words of others. I learn to "listen" for clunky notes that could be fine-tuned to make a piece of writing move gracefully forward.

Joni Mitchell's "Song To A Seagull" needs no honing. It is notable that, though the song is among her earliest work, it holds up today, both poetically and musically, even though she's moved on from folk to jazz, blues and even ballet.

Only she can say whether her dreams remain elusive or whether she has found the freedom she longed for. But her admirers can attest to her genius in expressing so eloquently the angst of an age.

With haiku-like simplicity, her words capture the universal yearning of young people with unconventional goals to break free. "Song To A Seagull" is not a complicated song or even an original sentiment. But Joni Mitchell's poetry carries a poignancy that most of us don't recognize until we are much older. When combined with her music, it is powerful:

> Fly silly seabird
> No dreams can possess you
> No voices can blame you for sun on your wings
> My gentle relations
> Have names they must call me
> For loving the freedom of all flying things
> My dreams with the seagull fly
> Out of reach out of cry

A somber guitar note thrums at the beginning of each line of the song, like a tolling bell. It sets an ominous cadence appropriate to the sense of loss in the lyrics. The dreamer fears what Mary Chapin Carpenter has called "time's unerring aim," the inexorable passage of opportunity. The repetitive note and elegiac chords lend an urgency to the fear that she will never find the freedom to pursue her art without distractions or judgment.

I was intrigued by the choice of "out of cry" for the chorus. The word "cry" evokes the keening of the gulls, turning a simple thought into a hymn to despair. "Out of hearing" just would not have the same effect. Or was the word "cry" chosen to signify "beyond tears"?

And what about the use of "silly" seagull? I pondered the choice of this adjective for days. The gull as a symbol seems so graceful and noble. Why not "snowy" seagull? Was the songwriter linking that trait to the gull because "silly" was one of the names that her "gentle relations" called her? Or is its meaning more obvious—that seagulls make a sound a lot like laughter and act clownish when stealing your lunch on land?

That is the beauty of poetry: it opens possibilities and leaves them to the reader's imagination. I don't want to over-analyze Joni Mitchell's word selection here, except that she, like me, is a self-professed lover of words. She dedicated this album to "Mr. Kratzman, who taught me to love words," a beloved teacher who encouraged her gift. She would not choose them cavalierly.

"She has a delicate pen, dipped in evanescent imagery never far from comprehension, but tickling to the senses and the intellect," wrote Robert Shelton in The New York Times on May 26, 1968. That review of the album *Song to A Seagull* must have made Mr. Kratzman proud.

Joni Mitchell's command of words shines brightest in the second verse, my favorite:

> I came to the city
> And lived like old Crusoe
> On an island of noise—in a cobblestone sea
> And the beaches were concrete
> And the stars paid a light bill [you've got to love this this line]
> And the blossoms hung false on their store window trees

Such indelible imagery has always set her apart from her contemporaries. She makes the city sound like a beautiful prison. I read somewhere that Joni was inspired to write this song when she poked her head out of her apartment window and noticed that her neighbor below had planted a window box with plastic flowers. Shades of "Big Yellow Taxi." Still, you can't miss the irony of her situation: the dreams that possessed her were attainable only by doing time on the island of noise. She was drawn to the unnatural landscape where the groundbreaking music-makers gathered, yet I believe the environment made her feel marooned rather than invigorated.

As a young woman, I found New York to be a place of excitement. But after a time viewing the sky through the slits between buildings and being assaulted by clamor and foul smells, I longed for greenery and peace. The girl in the song finds refuge at the beach, but does not find solace:

> Out of the city
> And down to the seaside
> To sun on my shoulders and wind in my hair
> But sandcastles crumble
> And hunger is human

> And humans are hungry for worlds they can't share

All who have had to put aside their dreams for mortgages or jobs—which is to say almost everyone—can relate to this sentiment. You have to eat, and, as the Rolling Stones bluntly put it, "You Can't Always Get What You Want." I love the assonant sounds within the repeated words "humans" and "hungry," a syllabic engine huffing along an arduous track.

The woman on the beach cries out in longing for the gull's independence and his ability to follow his nature. Soothing sibilant sounds in this passage convey the hissing of the waves and the serenity of the setting:

> I call to the seagull
> Who dives to the waters
> And catches his silver-fine dinner
> Alone

Here, the beachgoer imagines, the bird is flying free. In truth, the seagull is a slave to his silver-fine dinner. He wheels and swoops and dives for it not because it's fun. He does so at the relentless command of his gut. And he isn't always alone. Often, he must compete for the bounty.

Yet there is enviable simplicity in his behavior. Unlike the human on the beach, he is blissfully ignorant of conflicting needs.

In the final verse, the beachgoer mourns her lost illusions:

> Crying where are the footprints
> That danced on these beaches
> And the hands that cast wishes
> That sunk
> Like a stone
> My dreams with the seagulls fly
> Out of reach out of cry

So palpable is her hopelessness in this final verse that, the more I listened to it, the more I wondered if the woman on the beach had simply given up and walked into the ocean until she, too, sunk like a stone. My husband told me I was being too literal. Those ominous chords from Joni's guitar tell me I may be onto something, though.

I once wrote the following for my newspaper, which was sponsoring a poetry festival. It came from the heart and seems applicable here:

> Thank heaven for poets. When the rest of us are distracted by responsibility, they keep watch over what is important. They are consummate observers who see the music in ordinary things. They seek out simple truths and then, from the vast garden of language, pluck the perfect words to express their thoughts and feed the spirit.

The highest compliment I can pay to a piece of writing is to say, "I wish I'd written that."

I wish I'd written "Song To A Seagull."

RECONNECTING OURSELVES WITH NATURE

ROSIE GALLANT

My mother knew the birds. She knew them by name and by the expressions on their faces as they peeked through the windowsill of her beach house. Every morning she would draw them in her journal and call to tell me about the gatherings at her feeder, who stopped by and who she hadn't seen in awhile. She told me that she saw the spirit of each of her loved ones in her backyard birds. While I was away at school, I remained at home as the gentle pigeon cooing beside her sunflowers, and my brother, away in California, was the strong, independent blue jay that graced her afternoons with color and adventure. Her observations were brilliant, as if she was a seasoned naturalist, and when I came home, I knew exactly who each of the birds were, like they were characters from a story. To this day, I look back at her illustrations and I feel like I am looking through a photo album of family and friends.

My mother's love of the birds was much more than a hobby. She was physically confined by illness and found her freedom and vitality in the love of all flying things. The birds were her earthly messengers and with them she sent her dreams and hopes beyond the walls of her house and beyond the physical reality of her human body.

Joni's "Song To A Seagull" reminds me of the beauty and challenge in realizing our physical boundaries and accepting that nature, and all her messengers, have a freedom that we must learn to taste. Her imagery of a "cobblestone sea," "an island of noise," and "store window trees," speaks to me as both a lover of nature and a student of sustainability. I often feel trapped inside a material world. I know and witness few among my generation who stop to listen to the natural world around them and fewer willing to call out to the birds. I sense that we are growing weaker, less observant, less aware, and stepping further out of tune with the cadence of our Mother's drums.

I am confronted by a world unwilling to think beyond ourselves, to look to the forests for lessons, a world that has forgotten how to find our rhythm within a greater complex system and to ask Earth's messengers to help teach us the way. I sometimes wonder if we are content to be trapped, content to forgo our lessons in freedom and choose the less challenging route; we build our walls and never breach them.

With this in mind, I interpret "Song to a Seagull" as a longing to reconnect our human world with nature. Joni notes that "humans are hungry for worlds they can't share," and we are; we envy the liberty of birds. Our world is separate from the seagull's world, but it doesn't have to be. Our hunger is vain. In her song, Joni reconnects to the natural world and witnesses that, from the seagull's perspective, we have disappeared, we have confined ourselves. Like my mother did before her passing, I find comfort in Joni's song to the seagulls, in reconnecting ourselves to Earth and the birds. Through this song and countless others, I can feel that Joni's poetry is adaptive; it changes with the surrounding world. I am deeply inspired, as a student and a nature lover, by those in tune enough to speak to Earth's messengers, to ask for help and to sing them music. I am hopeful that our hunger will become consciousness and we will re-establish our bond with the world outside our walls.

CACTUS TREE

There's a man who's been out sailing
In a decade full of dreams
And he takes her to a schooner
And he treats her like a queen
Bearing beads from California
With their amber stones and green...
He has called her from the harbor
He has kissed her with his freedom
He has heard her off to starboard
In the breaking and the breathing
Of the water weeds
While she's so busy being free

There's a man who's climbed a mountain
And he's calling out her name
And he hopes her heart can hear 3 thousand miles
He calls again
He can think her there beside him
He can miss her just the same...
He has missed her in the forest
While he showed her all the flowers
And the branches sang the chorus
As he climbed the scaley towers
Of a forest tree
While she was somewhere being free

There's a man who's sent a letter
And he's waiting for reply
He has asked her of her travels
Since the day they said goodbye
He writes "Wish you were beside me
We can make it if we try..."

He has seen her at the office
With her name on all his papers
Thru the sharing of the profits
He will find it hard to shake her
From his memory
And she's so busy being free

There's a lady in the city
And she thinks she loves them all
There's the one who's thinking of her
There's the one who sometimes calls
There's the one who writes her letters
With his facts and figures scrawl...
She has brought them to her senses
They have laughed inside her laughter
Now she rallies her defenses
For she fears that one will ask her
For eternity
While she's so busy being free

There's a man who sends her medals
He is bleeding from the war
There's a jouster and a jester
And a man who owns a store
There's a drummer and a dreamer
And you know there may be more...
She will love them when she sees them
They will lose her if they follow
And she only means to please them
And her heart is full and hollow
Like a cactus tree
While she's so busy being free

"LIKE A CACTUS TREE": COMING OF AGE WITH JONI MITCHELL'S MUSIC

RICHARD FLYNN

The first time I saw Joni was November of '68—Thanksgiving week in the U.S. I sat with my parents at a table next to the small stage at the Cellar Door, a 192-seat dark café that used to be at the corner of 34th and M Streets in Washington, D.C. I was thirteen.

This was not the first time I had been to that long-gone, now-legendary club. I was obsessed with music and had previously convinced my parents to take me to see such musical heroes as Judy Collins and Ian & Sylvia there. But I knew that, for me, Joni Mitchell was in a category of her own, even in late 1968 when all I had to base my judgment on were the songs I knew from other artists' versions and those on her debut LP, *Joni Mitchell* aka *Song to a Seagull*.

The previous spring, in late March, I had taken a D.C. Transit bus to the Soul Shack at 12th and G to buy that album, an album I had been anticipating for well over a year. A privileged child, I had been enamored of folk music (or, more accurately, the music of the pop-folk revival) even before my family moved to Washington, D.C., in 1963, when I was eight—the same year I began guitar lessons. I shared the third floor attic of our Friendship Heights house with my brother, where every night I listened to Dick Cerri's Music Americana on WAVA FM, learning about new singers and songwriters: Tom Paxton, Tom Rush, Eric Andersen, Buffy Sainte Marie, Ian & Sylvia, Dave Van Ronk and more. I subscribed to *Sing Out!* magazine. Long before I ever heard Joni Mitchell sing or play, her songs had already struck a chord deep in me. The songs I knew from other artists—"Urge for Going," "The Circle Game," "Both Sides Now," "Michael from Mountains" and "Song to a Seagull"—were wise beyond my years, certainly. They spoke in frank terms about how idealism is inevitably tempered by experience. They were tough and uncompromising in their honesty. Joni remarked to Michelle Mercer, "The people who get the most out my music see themselves in it." I saw myself in her songs before I had heard her sing them and sensed that they, like other poetry, would offer sustenance for future years.

So, that March I listened repeatedly to Joni's tale of coming to the city "to live like old Crusoe" and leaving the city in Nathan La Franeer's "coach" to escape to the seaside (going on her own rather than waiting, like poor "Marcie," for someone to take her). I let that music wash over me and comfort me days later as, from my privileged, white neighborhood, I watched the firelit, smoky sky on the horizon as the city burned in the aftermath of the Martin Luther King, Jr. assassination.

Like most thirteen year olds, I experienced a mass of conflicting, contradictory emotions. My awakening social conscience forced me to put my convictions into action—I had already begun stuffing envelopes for Gene McCarthy's Presidential bid and marched on Solidarity Day that June—but it also caused me to chafe against my position of privilege. I unsuccessfully resisted my parents' bid to place me in an exclusive boy's prep school that fall, but I was thrilled that their wealth provided me with a new Martin D-28 that same year.

Armed with that beautiful guitar, I recognized that in order to play Joni Mitchell's songs, I had to detune it and discovered open E. Capoing up to F#, I figured out how to play along to "Cactus Tree," the wisest song on the first album, and one that sums up, acknowledges and embodies the complexities and contradictions of city and seaside, isolation and connection, love and liberation in the songs that lead up to it.

At thirteen, I was ready for "Cactus Tree" precisely because it spoke of things beyond my experience. I was a melancholy, sensitive boy, with a romantic streak a mile wide, and I think what I needed most was the toughness of the song, a toughness reinforced by the third person narration. "Cactus Tree" demonstrates that Joni already understood at twenty-four that innocence and experience are, as Blake tells us, "two contrary states of the human soul" that coexist within us simultaneously—and also that hearts could be paradoxically "full and hollow." It has always annoyed me to hear the early Joni characterized as a flower child or hippie chick, to see her early work characterized, as Larry David Smith does, as a "hippie manifesto."

Regardless of the period-style album artwork, there is nothing precious or fey about the songs on *Song To A Seagull*: the overall narrative and Joni's gift for the deft, poetic character sketch are already well-developed. She displays a remarkable maturity and detachment in her employment of first-person singular and plural speakers, and her imagery is concrete and specific in a way that distinguishes her already from most of her contemporaries. Though perhaps more detached than on *Blue* or *For the Roses*, the personae and the subjects of *Song to a Seagull* speak, or rather sing, across the boundaries of gender and of age.

The three men depicted in the first three stanzas of "Cactus Tree" seem to offer different romantic models. The charmingly seductive sailor bears nearly irresistible gifts, including the kiss of freedom, but of course it is his freedom—that is, freedom on his terms and therefore potentially threatening to the unnamed female protagonist. The romantic allure of being treated "like a queen" gives way to another feminine archetype (or stereotype), the mermaid. To give in to a "decade full of dreams" might mean submission to an oceanic feeling, but the "she" who is so busy being free seems to find herself wanting boundaries.

The man "who's climbed a mountain" is all longing and desire, and his picture of the protagonist is almost dependent on her absence: "He can think her there beside him / He can miss her just the same...." In fact, he seems to miss her even when she is present: "He has missed her in the forest / While he showed her all the flowers." The modification to the refrain underscores her absence: "She's so busy being free" becomes, in this instance, "While she was somewhere being free." The man is also off somewhere in his own world and, unlike the sailor, he has erected insurmountable boundaries; one imagines that he is like "Michael from Mountains": "You want to know all / But his mountains have called so you never do."

In contrast to these hopeless romantics, the "man who's sent a letter" is clearly a figure from the past, one with whom the protagonist maintains a business relationship. Unlike the bohemian lovers in stanzas one and two, this figure seemed to me to be a particularly undesirable model of masculinity. The lyrics "He has seen her at the office / With her name on all his papers / Thru the sharing of the profits" underscored for me not only the price my parents' unstable marriage exacted on our family, but also my own uneasiness about the ways in which our affluence was bought at the price of our family's increasing estrangement. We were all less than pleased "to be a part of the arrangement."

The song pivots brilliantly as "she" becomes the focal character in stanza four: the "lady in the city" who "thinks she loves them all." The men of the preceding three stanzas are summarized or sketched in three shorthand phrases: "the one who's thinking of her," "the one who sometimes calls" and "the one who writes her letters / With his facts and figures scrawl." Seemingly in control, "she has brought them to her senses" in a gesture that is at once rational and sensual. Somewhat ambivalently, she recognizes that she is in control in that she may use them for her pleasure, but also sees that control as short-lived. The lovers return to haunt her; they "have laughed inside her laughter" in such a way that she must "rall[y] her defenses" to avoid being confined for eternity. Because it was not socially acceptable in the late 1960s for a woman singer to simply be stone free or like a rolling stone, claiming agency for the protagonist of "Cactus Tree" is complicated.

In a 1968 interview in Dave Wilson's Broadside of Boston, Joni says that she wrote "Cactus Tree" after seeing the Dylan movie *Don't Look Back*, which "left a big impression on [her]." The final stanza of "Cactus Tree" recapitulates the portraits of the men who have appeared in the song, but they are reduced to types (wounded soldier, jouster, jester, storeowner, drummer, dreamer) as if perhaps the protagonist could herself display the cool cruelty of the Dylan who cuts everyone down to size in Pennebaker's film. The narrator/singer, however, sees the vulnerability and defensiveness in this stance. Freedom has a price—one's heart will be full and hollow, but giving up freedom might just empty out that heart altogether. Better to live and love unconventionally. And don't look back. Still, like the singer of "The Gallery," the protagonist of "Cactus Tree" chooses gentleness over cruelty.

The second time I saw Joni, at Constitution Hall in D.C. on January 29, 1974, I had just turned nineteen and was more experienced than I wished to be. I had just begun college at George Washington University, but I had spent four months at the beginning of 1972, and later the greater part of the summer of 1973, as a "Trouble Child"—"up in a sterilized room / where they let you be crazy." The version of "Cactus Tree" from this period, as the *Miles of Aisles* recording attests, is emotionally definitive. Performed a whole step lower than the 1968 recording, Joni's more weathered, more expressive vocals are as gut-wrenching now as they were to me then. The performance is less defiant, wiser and ultimately heartbreaking. From my own personal experience (and through Joni's greater command as a performer), the costs of love—that "repetitious danger," "the greatest poison and medicine of all"—became clear to a still-damaged teenager, alone in the dark concert hall.

The last time I saw Joni was August of '79, at Merriweather Post Pavilion, with her most amazing band ever. I was twenty-four, the age at which Joni recorded her first album. "Cactus Tree" had dropped out of her concert repertoire after the 1974 tour. A number of fairweather fans had fallen by the wayside. (I remained and remain loyal.) That show featured "Amelia"— a first-person cri de couer that is in many ways even more powerful than "Cactus Tree." The singer, a kindred spirit to "the ghost of aviation," Amelia Earhart, "check[s] into the Cactus Tree Motel to shower off the dust" where she sleeps "on the strange pillows of [her] wanderlust." When *Hejira* appeared in 1976, I had become as serious about poetry as I had always been about music. I was a senior, studying with the poet Marilyn Hacker and writing a senior thesis on the work of Muriel Rukeyser. I was particularly taken by Rukeyser's poem "Double Ode" (1976) in which she comes to terms with "the black... mysteries" of her rejecting parents, who nevertheless taught her "the eternal double music male and female." Rukeyer repeats an incantation three times in the poem:

Pay attention to what they tell you to forget.

Pay attention to what they tell you to forget.
Pay attention to what they tell you to forget.

Though I had largely succeeded in putting myself together again, *Hejira* spoke to me with the same intensity as Rukeyser's poem, and it taught me to pay attention and to remember. I spent countless hours in the dark listening through headphones. I heard the six men of the last stanza of "Cactus Tree" transform into "six white vapor trails across the bleak terrain": "It was the hexagram of the heavens / It was the strings of my guitar / Amelia, it was just a false alarm."

This singer, who once "looked at clouds from both sides now," feels she has "spent her whole life in clouds at icy altitudes." Nevertheless, "like Icarus ascending / On beautiful foolish arms," she can't quite bring herself to become a permanent "defector from the petty wars" ("Hejira").

"People will tell you where they've gone / They'll tell you where to go / But till you get there yourself you never really know," Joni sings in "Amelia." The initial image of six jet planes from the first stanza of the song returns in the last, in her dream "of 747s / Over geometric farms." The singer has learned to "hide the hurt," but still "the road leads cursed and charmed." In the final stanza, the singer of "Amelia" looks up and down, forward and back. She is the woman of "Cactus Tree," with fewer illusions. Yet, as I hear her wise counsel to herself and Amelia, it is no longer "just" a false alarm; in the final refrain "false alarms" are joined by "dreams." The woman in "Cactus Tree" has been there and back, she is road-weary and wiser, her heart is still "full and hollow," but in her search for both love and freedom, like me, she has "a dream to fly."

I DON'T KNOW WHERE I STAND

Funny day
Looking for laughter and finding it there
Sunny day
Braiding wild flowers and leaves in my hair
I picked up a pencil and wrote "I love you"
In my finest hand
I wanted to send it
But I don't know where I stand

Telephone
Even the sound of your voice is still new
All alone
In California and talking to you
And feeling too foolish and strange to say
The words that I had planned
I guess it's too early
'Cause I don't know where I stand

Crickets call
Courting their ladies in star-dappled green
Thickets tall
Until the morning comes up like a dream
All muted and misty
So drowsy now
I'll take what sleep I can
I know that I miss you
But I don't know where I stand

I DON'T KNOW WHERE I STAND

JUNE BISANTZ

At any moment during the last four decades, I could have recited the lyrics of "I Don't Know Where I Stand" from memory. Though until recently I hadn't heard the song for many years, it has remained vibrantly alive in both my memory and imagination. In this song, as in all her work, Joni Mitchell creates multi-dimensional poetry that is emotionally, musically and visually resonant and timeless. Her poetry has been a great gift—demonstrating the combined power of disparate forms of creative expression to produce a cohesive, honest, emotional whole.

> Telephone
> Even the sound of your voice is still new
> All alone
> In California and talking to you
> And feeling too foolish and strange to say
> The words that I had planned
> I guess it's too early
> 'Cause I don't know where I stand

Just typing those words brings chills. They perfectly describe not just my story, but the story of many women. We experience romantic connection immediately—from the very first moment. Far, far ahead of the game, we can only wait for time to reveal the truth of what we have gotten ourselves into and the reality of where we stand.

The poetry of this song deals eloquently with the excitement and anxiety associated with going somewhere new, of becoming someone new. Exuberant and timid all at once, "feeling too foolish and strange to say / The words that I had planned / I guess it's too early / 'Cause I don't know where I stand." The message seems to be: embrace and celebrate love, but watch your step, your heart, your happiness—until time inevitably lets you know exactly where you stand.

The poetry of "I Don't Know Where I Stand" is also multi-layered and complex. It is as much about the creative experience as it is about love, beautifully describing the longing, hope, self-doubt and brutal honesty underlying all creative endeavors. In the creative struggle, as in love, you learn where you stand over time, by taking risks, by being strong, holding on and staying in the struggle. Finally, "All muted and misty / So drowsy now / I'll take what sleep I can." What else can we do but anticipate, hope, risk and wait to know where we stand.

THE FIDDLE AND THE DRUM

And so once again
My dear Johnny, my dear friend
And so once again you are fightin' us all
And when I ask you why
You raise your sticks and cry, and I fall
Oh, my friend
How did you come
To trade the fiddle for the drum

You say I have turned
Like the enemies you've earned
But I can remember
All the good things you are
And so I ask you please
Can I help you find the peace and the star
Oh, my friend
What time is this
To trade the handshake for the fist

And so once again
Oh, America my friend
And so once again
You are fighting us all
And when we ask you why
You raise your sticks and cry and we fall
Oh, my friend
How did you come
To trade the fiddle for the drum

You say we have turned
Like the enemies you've earned
But we can remember
All the good things you are
And so we ask you please
Can we help you find the peace and the star
Oh my friend
We have all come
To fear the beating of your drum!

THE FIDDLE AND THE DRUM

NATHAN WISE

The single most stirring performance of an anti-war song I ever witnessed occurred at Yale in 1968, when the great Theodore Bikel concluded a concert with the bitter, war-weary, "Johnny I Hardly Knew Ye." Playing his signature folk guitar, Bikel sang the verse, "Oh ye haven't an arm and ye haven't a leg, hurroo, hurroo," with an aching pathos that brought silence to the hall filled with rapt students, and then, with a piercing staccato that punctuated his anger, he began the final chorus a cappella, striking the face of his guitar with hollow thumps imitative of drumbeats: "With your guns and drums and drums and guns, hurroo, hurroo," and I could feel the emotion well up in my throat. The Vietnam War was at its height, student protests had begun at Columbia the previous year, L.B.J. had been driven from a second term by his tragic foreign policy and Nixon would soon be in the White House. We would listen as our birthdays were read out as part of a new draft lottery. My number was 161.

"The Fiddle And The Drum" is Joni Mitchell's anti-war masterpiece, and it is pure poetry. She performs it a cappella, in fact, which allows for an almost free-form pace, rising and falling and finally building to the last five, extended notes, " bea-ting-of-your-drum"—each tone stressed equally, like a funereal drum, or the frightening sound of Fate pounding on the door, as Beethoven's Fifth Symphony has sometimes been described. The performance seems to be a recitation, rather than a song, which enhances its poetic quality. It is spare, symbolic and allegorical, like the poetry of William Blake, which makes it even more remarkable, because it comes from the same pen that also gave us the rich, anthropomorphic naturalism of "Urge for Going," with imagery as vivid as Robert Frost's or Edna St. Vincent Millay's. I truly believe that Joni Mitchell deserves a place among such exalted geniuses of poetry.

Mitchell chooses to begin "The Fiddle And The Drum" with the perfect words—"And so once again"—because it implies the continuation of something. In this case, it's war. There's an ennui and sadness in the phrase, which will turn to anger and defiance by the time she describes the trade of "the handshake for the fist." I love those opening words, too, for their contrast with historical techniques, which grip the audience's attention suddenly, as with the Old English exclamatory "Hwaet" (which I've seen translated as "Lo," but which really meant more like "Be quiet and put down your cups of mead, because I'm about to recite") or William Butler Yeats's great "Leda and the Swan," which engages the reader immediately with the violence of "A sudden blow." No, Mitchell wants us to feel a sense of inevitability and inescapability and, worst of all, futility. Fate isn't knocking at the door; it's Truth that has walked in, uninvited. That's the poetic power (and the poet's wisdom) in that little three letter conjunction "And" as the initial word: it doesn't grip you instantly, it seduces you insidiously, and that's why Mitchell uses it. Her "Johnny" is a departure from the universal soldier in the nineteenth-century Irish original, "Johnny I Hardly Knew Ye," who is the hapless victim of war. Mitchell's Johnny is a new name for Uncle Sam when the Canadian poet says, "My dear Johnny, my dear friend," and later, "Oh, America my friend." As such, this Johnny is the protagonist, and is fearsome in his preference for "the fist" over "the handshake." Mitchell has turned "Johnny I Hardly Knew Ye" on its head, and the effect is shattering. She is mindful, too, that Union and Confederate troops transformed the original song into "When Johnny Comes Marchin' Home." It was a jingoistic adaptation, reflective of each side's bellicose self-assuredness during the 1860s, in which Johnny is now a hero and a victor, rather than the battered, multi-faceted victim (that the Irish of the 1820s and Theodore Bikel in the '60s) mourned as war's ugly, truncated aftermath. The melody even emerges later as an effective, ironic refrain in Billy Wilder's brilliant P.O.W. film, *Stalag 17*, which was set in World War II.

Toward the end of his unhappy life, the great poet Edgar Allan Poe published an esoteric but fascinating essay on prosody entitled "The Rationale of Verse." In this piece, he provided a dense analysis of meter that is difficult to slog through today, but valuable, because I cannot think of a poet who was more musical than Poe ("The tintinnabulation of the bells, the bells, the bells") without actually having himself been a songwriter. I can definitely imagine Poe rapping a walking stick on the floor, intoning the iambi, anapests and dactyls of "And so once again, my dear Johnny, my dear friend." The next line repeats the same meter and is followed by a lovely, almost Shakespearean iambic hexameter "And when I ask you why/You raise your sticks and cry" accelerating the movement and building to the climactic question, which, after all, is the poet's central, unanswered perplexity, and the very heart of the piece: "How did you come / To trade the fiddle for the drum?" The essential, contrasting words "fiddle" and "drum" are also worth pondering, for their power is definitive, symbolic and rhythmic, all at once. The word, "fiddle" has the short vowel sounds and the quick syllables, imitative of the instrument itself and its use as an accompaniment to dance, merriment and leisure. Visit New York's majestic Metropolitan Museum of Art and wander through the glorious musical instrument collection, and you will see (among other things) the violin family in its entirety, from the stately contrabass at the deep end, to the tiniest little fiddles (called kits), which could be kept in a vest pocket to accompany a jig. Now contrast that image with the resonant monosyllable and extended vowel sound of the word "drum" and you will recognize that the use of these two musical instruments offers symbolic distinctions as well as linguistic differences that add the necessary dynamic dimension to the simplicity of the words themselves.

The words "handshake" and "fist," which replace "fiddle" and "drum" at the end of the second stanza or verse, can also be looked at that way. "Handshake" has an openness to it, with the sounds of the letters "a" and the crisp consonants. "Fist," though, is closed, sibilant and quick—it seems to allow for neither response nor argument nor hope for a peaceful resolution. This juxtaposition suits the poet's intent perfectly. The fact that Johnny raises "sticks" (in the plural, rather than the singular) emphasizes the image that Johnny is a multitude or a nation, and not simply an individual.

The poet, with the mastery of simplicity, has once again shown the artistry of language that elevates "The Fiddle And The Drum" to poetry so well-crafted as to enrich Mitchell's remarkable opus beyond measure. It is the simplicity of the poet's message, and the purity of its execution, that focuses the attention, at last, on the greatest truth of the piece—the final words, "We have all come / To fear the beating of your drum!" As mentioned at the outset, but seen now as the conclusion of a poem rather than a song, these words receive five stressed syllables at the end, in dreadful and frightening foreboding. Although Mitchell assures America that "we can remember / All the good things you are" (note that she maintains the optimism of the present tense of "you are"), it is nevertheless clear that Johnny's course is a mighty, earthbound steamroller compared with Mitchell's ethereal "the peace and the star." Vietnam would last another six years. Its specter continues to stalk my generation to this day.

BOTH SIDES NOW

Rows and floes of angel hair
And ice cream castles in the air
And feather canyons everywhere
I've looked at clouds that way...
But now they only block the sun
They rain and snow on ev'ryone
So many things I would have done
But clouds got in my way!
I've looked at clouds from both sides now
From up and down, and still somehow
It's cloud illusions I recall
I really don't know clouds at all

Moons and Junes and Ferris wheels
The dizzy dancing way you feel
As ev'ry fairy tale comes real
I've looked at love that way
But now it's just another show
You leave 'em laughing when you go
And if you care, don't let them know
Don't give yourself away!
I've looked at love from both sides now
From give and take, and still somehow
It's love's illusions I recall
I really don't know love at all

Tears and fears and feeling proud
To say "I love you" right out loud
Dreams and schemes and circus crowds
I've looked at life that way...

But now old friends are acting strange

They shake their heads, and they tell me that I've changed

Well something's lost, but something's gained

In living every day!

I've looked at life from both sides now

From win and lose, and still somehow

It's life's illusions I recall

I really don't know life at all

BOTH SIDES NOW

FELICITY HARLEY

1969's *Clouds* is the second album by Joni Mitchell. It has little more than Mitchell's voice and solo acoustic guitar for accompaniment, employing chords chromatically related by tritones or thirds. Mitchell wrote "Both Sides Now" for others but sung it herself for the first time on this album. It is one of her most famous songs and has been sung by multiple artists. In 1970, *Clouds* won the Grammy for best folk album of 1969.

I first heard "Both Sides Now" in 1970, a year after Joni Mitchell recorded it. We were about the same age. I was an aspiring writer and poet and had just immigrated to the U.S. from the U.K. She was from somewhere else just like me.

> Rows and floes of angel hair
> And ice cream castles in the air
> And feather canyons everywhere
>
> Moons and Junes and Ferris wheels
> The dizzy dancing way you feel
> As ev'ry fairy tale comes real
>
> Tears and fears and feeling proud
> To say "I love you" right out loud
> Dreams and schemes and circus crowds

Ribbons of colored words that run through the essentially sad and defiant fabric of her song:

> So many things I would have done
> But clouds got in my way!
>
> But now it's just another show
> you leave 'em laughing when you go
> And if you care don't let them know
> Don't give yourself away!
>
> I've looked at love from both sides now
> From give and take, and still somehow
> It's love's illusions I recall
> I really don't know love at all

There she stood, vibrant, her sweet and lyrical voice soaring with just an acoustic guitar to keep the beat. As I listened, I thought... what did she or I really know about life or love anyway?

Recently I heard the same song, recorded in 2004 on her compilation album *Dreamland*. On this track, the voice of a much older woman sings pensively, slowly, throatily echoed by the wandering and reflective notes of a trumpet:

I've looked at life from both sides now
From win and lose, and still somehow
It's life's illusions I recall
I really don't know life at all

This time, as I listen to her lyrics, I know exactly what she means: do any of us really know life at all, and can any of us guess what the years will bring, and if we could would we want to?

Joni Mitchell came out of the '60s. This was a period of time for artists in the US that combined romanticism with revolution. Mitchell caught the bug, and while some of her songs relate to social change, many express this yearning for change through her own personal lens. The '50s in post-war America were all about conformity and prosperity. Necessarily so, because a country that had thought it was beyond the grasp of the huge war that overtook Europe at the beginning of the 1940s was soon engulfed. Americans had to make sacrifices, and when the troops came home they were ready to live the American Dream. Boxlike suburbs sprang up with June Cleaver on one end and Pinkie Lee at the other. Washing machines, television and the motor car became the new American mantra. However, even in the '50s, the emptiness of these values had gripped a whole generation of people including Kerouac, James Dean, Marlon Brando—rebels without a cause, who were alienated and sensed that something was missing.

In the 1960s, the great Bob Dylan, Joan Baez, Motown and even Elvis unleashed a flood of truth and passion in their songs that reflected the anti-war protests, the civil rights movement and a general rebellion against middle class restraints that were going on in America at the time. Mitchell was among these folk; while I do not think she is particularly politically motivated in this song, she seems personally rebellious. She clearly doesn't want to accept the middle class, 1950s definition of love, the one that could end, for a white woman, in a dead-end suburban marriage, like those so well described by Marilyn French in *The Women's Room*. She seems to see this definition of love as a "grand illusion." She indicates that she'll look for something else, something that is more romantic, more spiritual perhaps, and something that is not defined by the bourgeois, middle class fifties culture in which I grew up. And, in the end, she tells us clearly what her choices are despite the consequences and the risks:

But now old friends are acting strange
They shake their heads, and they tell me that I've changed
Well something's lost, but something's gained
In living every day!

As she croons the last lines of her song, you believe that, even in this modern world of the youthfully arrogant Mark Zuckerberg and Facebook, the human heart and soul are a mystery that we will never be able to fully solve or digitalize. And for that, I am eternally grateful to her and to us, the revolutionaries of the '60s.

FOR FREE

I slept last night in a good hotel
I went shopping today for jewels
The wind rushed around in the dirty town
And the children let out from the schools
I was standing on a noisy corner
Waiting for the walking green
Across the street he stood
And he played real good
On his clarinet
For free

Now me I play for fortune
And those velvet curtain calls
I've got a black limousine and two gentlemen
Escorting me to the halls
I play if you have the money
Or if you're a friend to me
But the one man band
By the quick lunch stand
He was playing real good
For free

He was
Playing like a fallen angel
Playing like a rising star
Playing for a hat full of nothing
to the honking of the cars

Nobody stopped to hear him
Though he played so sweet and high
They knew he had never been on their TV
So they passed his good music by
I meant to go over and ask for a song
Maybe put on a harmony...
I heard his refrain
As the signal changed
He was playing real good
For free

PASSED BY/FOR FREE

WINKY GORDON

I find the song terribly sad. It conjures images of aloneness—the desire and inability to connect. I see a lone crow, a man in a shack by himself, a solitary dog in the dirt outside and empty town. The lyrics and music are beautiful, melancholy and filled with the ghost of remorse. I see myself in each character and have played all three parts: the narrator who doesn't connect, the inattentive crowd and the solo musician giving away his gift in the middle of chaos. The richness and power of this song-poem, to me, is in the questions it causes me to ask.

I imagine a narrator cloaked in the habit of seeking security and certainty. She has money enough for jewels and good hotels, and is guarded by her escorts and limousine. Her audiences adore her and woo her with curtain calls. She has success. But she also has desire that is not allowed to blossom. Her layers of protection, real and imagined, keep her from connecting with the street musician whose song and freedom she admires. She does not receive this gift of communion.

How do I keep myself apart, and what desires do I deny?

The inattentive crowd—they simply pass by the beauty the musician offers. He plays on the street corner, right under their noses, and they miss it. His free, sweet song is lifted up and they don't notice. They keep themselves separate from a moment of possibility.

What are the gems, who are the people, where are the places I deprive myself of when I simply pass them by? It makes me think of the secrets of the soil and the stories of the people I work with; how easily I miss the opportunity to really know these things.

The musician is alone but not lonely. He does not wait for permission, or certainty, or for someone to lead the way. He is free because he is not separate. He joins his music and becomes the spectacle, revealed and vulnerable. He moves right into the depth of his gift and allows the song to direct him there, right there, beyond the limit of the predictable and the known.

How can I let go into the unknown? How might I let myself be moved by and freer with my own gifts?

LADIES OF THE CANYON

Trina wears her wampum beads
She fills her drawing book with line
Sewing lace on widows' weeds
And filigree on leaf and vine
Vine and leaf are filigree
And her coat's a secondhand one
Trimmed in antique luxury
She is a lady of the canyon

Annie sits you down to eat
She always makes you welcome in
Cats and babies 'round her feet
And all are fat and none are thin
None are thin and all are fat
She may bake some brownies today
Saying you are welcome back
She is another canyon lady

Estrella circus girl
Comes wrapped in songs and gypsy shawls
Songs like tiny hammers hurled
At beveled mirrors in empty halls
Empty halls and beveled mirrors
Sailing seas and climbing banyans
Come out for a visit here
To be a lady of the canyon

Trina takes her paints and her threads
And she weaves a pattern all her own
Annie bakes her cakes and her breads
And she gathers flowers for her home

For her home she gathers flowers
And Estrella, dear companion
Colors up the sunshine hours
Pouring music down the canyon

Coloring the sunshine hours
They are the ladies of the canyon

TRINA WEARS HER WAMPUM BEADS

TRINA ROBBINS

It was 1968, and the worst time to be in New York was February, so I was in Los Angeles for a month, staying at the home of friends in the Canyon. I looked up David Crosby, who'd been my good friend back when I lived in LA, and of course he was in the Canyon, too. He was producing Joni Mitchell's first album; they had already been an item, but Joni had moved on, and David still harbored no-longer-requited love in his heart for her. Who wouldn't? Long-legged and slim, with her long golden hair falling about her shoulders like a veil, Joni was everything I was not: short and stubby, with curly hair when straight hair was so in vogue. And her voice! Pouring from her throat like light beams were crystalline notes that could make a lion lie down at her feet and purr.

"Trina wears her wampum beads"

Actually, they were love beads, just hippie love beads, but poets get to use poetic license, and wampum beads sounds so much more romantic.

My boyfriend had flown down from New York to stay with me in the Canyon—not a good idea, as his close proximity was getting on my nerves. Another bad idea was taking acid together while our friends were out, but we cluelessly did that anyway. And, as we were coming down, my friends returned with their friends, a man and a woman whom I had already met. The woman, whose name is lost in the mists of time (What was your name? Will you read this and come forth, that I may thank you again?), said, "I'm glad you're here, Trina. I made this for you." And she presented me with the beads.

I put them on and didn't take them off until one day they broke.

"She fills her drawing book with line"

There wasn't a time when I hadn't been drawing. In 1966, I looked at a copy of *The East Village Other*, one of the first underground newspapers, and saw a one-page psychedelic comic strip called Gentle's Tripout signed by someone called Panzika (later I found out that Panzika was a woman), and realized that the little drawings of people on paper that I produced were actually comics.

I had a boutique in New York's Lower East Side, sitting at a sewing machine all day, producing little mini dresses of velvet and lace. I made a jacket out of American flags for the editor of EVO, and in return I got free advertising for my boutique, which took the form of a comic so spacey that few people realized it was actually an ad for a shop. I carried a sketch pad and magic markers around with me at all times, and just sat and drew—sometimes comics, sometimes leaf and vine and filigree.

"Sewing lace on widows' weeds"

See above: the boutique. You could still get ancient art nouveau ornamentation cheap. Once, someone walked into my shop and sold me a huge bag filled with fin de siècle buckles and buttons for ten dollars, and I sewed them onto the little minis I made. The same went for beautiful handmade lace. After Joni wrote those lyrics, I was so grateful that I made her a simple, black mini dress with the only ornamentation being a piece of antique lace that I turned into a pocket.

"And filigree on leaf and vine"

Vine and leaf are filigree
See above: the sketchbook.

"And her coat's a secondhand one
Trimmed in antique luxury"

Ah, The Coat!

I had moved to New York from Los Angeles in the summer of 1966, and almost immediately rented a storefront and started making my clothes. I did pretty well until February, 1967, when I discovered that, in New York, nobody buys anything in February. Everybody has spent all their money on Christmas, and they're all too depressed because they've had three months of snow and cold. And the weather is so rotten in February that most folks don't even leave their homes except to forage for necessities like food.

That year, the big fashion fad in the cold weather states was vintage fur coats, which people bought pretty cheaply in vast warehouses stacked with furs. Someone introduced me to the owner of one of those warehouses, and when his customers wanted their coats altered, he sent them to me. I survived for the month of February, 1967, by altering furs: shortening them to mini lengths, removing their shoulder pads, desecrating them in all manner of ways in the name of fashion. A woman brought in a three-quarter length skunk coat and left it with me. She'd be back, she told me, to discuss what she wanted done to it. By March, when she hadn't returned, I made it mine. I didn't do anything to it— kept the Joan Crawford-style shoulder pads so that it was as wide as it was long—and wearing it I looked like a giant fuzzy die.

Then, when February rolled around again in '68, knowing there was no point in staying in New York, I sublet my apartment for a month to a rock musician (Where are you, Jessie?), let a friend stay in my storefront (Alison Diaz, where are you now?), and fled to the warmth of Los Angeles, bringing the coat with me.

"She is a lady of the canyon."

Well, for a month.

BIG YELLOW TAXI

They paved paradise
And put up a parking lot
With a pink hotel, a boutique
And a swinging hot spot
Don't it always seem to go
That you don't know what you've got
Till it's gone
They paved paradise
And put up a parking lot

They took all the trees
Put 'em in a tree museum
And they charged the people
An arm and a leg just to see 'em
Don't it always seem to go
That you don't know what you've got
Till it's gone
They paved paradise
And put up a parking lot!

Hey farmer farmer
Put away that DDT now
Give me spots on my apples
But leave me the birds and the bees
Please!
Don't it always seem to go
That you don't know what you've got
Till it's gone
They paved paradise
And put up a parking lot

Late last night
I heard the screen door slam
And a big yellow taxi came
And took away my old man
Don't it always seem to go
That you don't know what you've got
Till it's gone
They paved paradise
And put up a parking lot!

They paved paradise
And put up a parking lot!

BIG YELLOW TAXI, OR THE DEMISE OF THE NATURAL WORLD

RAVI SHANKAR

"I wrote 'Big Yellow Taxi' on my first trip to Hawaii. I took a taxi to the hotel and when I woke up the next morning, I threw back the curtains and saw these beautiful green mountains in the distance. Then, I looked down and there was a parking lot as far as the eye could see, and it broke my heart... this blight on paradise. That's when I sat down and wrote the song."
-Joni Mitchell, being interviewed by Alan McDougall (1972)

On the website "Police Vehicles of Canada," or rather "Les véhicules de police du Canada," since the site is nearly entirely in French, one can find a photo of a Toronto cop car—a Chrysler circa 1969, painted mustard yellow—and there have been some who posited that this distinctive lemony appendage of authority was the source of inspiration for Joni Mitchell's song "Big Yellow Taxi," though I'd present as counterargument the fact that, by then, she'd stopped busking in the streets of Toronto and had moved to New York. Nonetheless, this car, which whisks away her old man in the song, has a foreboding resonance that uses the poetic device of metonymy, the car standing in for the big, anonymous institutions that would legislate our movements, and would trademark and sell air if they could.

Though it might reveal a bit too much about my proclivities at the time, I admit I was first introduced to the song through the East Bay's punk rock band Pinhead Gunpowder's fast-paced cover version—a very Green Day-esque rendering that was an odd but perpetual favorite at the jukebox of the Comet, the little dive bar with the photo booth where I lived in San Francisco. I always thought the track was catchy, but never really put much thought into its origins because back then I was interested in much more crucial issues, like making sure I could chat up the comely art students wandering the Haight-Ashbury or that I had an appropriately-chosen, hipster-sanctioned favorite taqueria in the Mission.

Then, years later studying poetry in graduate school in New York City, I was sitting in Riverside Park when out of the open window of a big yellow cab, of all things, I heard some lyrics that made me swoon for an instant, familiar but not quite recongizable. We've all had such minute, transformational moments, like when the echo of a perfectly balanced pinot noir reverberates in the throat and back onto the palate with the ghost of fruit once hung swollen on the vine, and maybe we could have such moments each and every day if we only we could attune our daily awareness to aesthetic vision, as Joni Mitchell has done throughout her life. For me, it was one of those jarring moments that reminded me how sweet it is to be alive: sitting in a park with a volume of, I don't know, John Berryman or H.D., creased open on my lap when a snatch of a song wafted by to infuse the afternoon with a new mood, one of longing and heightened awareness to the swaying canopy of leaves around me. I was struck, as if by déjà vu, and it was only later that I realized I had heard the song before, albeit in a much different form.

They took all the trees and put them in a tree museum, then charged the people a dollar and a half just to see them were the lines that emanated from the cab that moment in the park when the traffic light changed and the cab charged downtown in a burst of black smoke. Jolted, I immediately looked around to remind myself of where I was sitting and, more existentially, who and what I was. It's funny in retrospect that for someone who considers language the most precise tool we have at our disposal to give shape to the abstract and to the inchoate, I can't remember for the life of me what book I was reading, yet I have this aural memory of that snippet of song, as lucid to me now as on that day I heard it. Or maybe I can only remember the memory of the experience and not the experience itself. Or maybe I invented the whole episode in specific detail because that's what listening to Joni does to me—makes me feel like each new now is a chance to imaginatively reconstruct the world, in spite of war and atrocity, selfish disregard and environmental blight, those aspects of human behavior that one must always speak out against, lest they overwhelm civilization.

Somehow, for me, "Big Yellow Taxi" illuminates the environmental tipping point our culture has been approached at breakneck speed more persuasively than something polemical like Rachel Carson's "Silent Spring" or some of Greenpeace's heavy-handedtactics. Joni's sensuous alto resonates with more power and lasting relevance than the shrill debates about climate change on Capital Hill. Part of the song's power is the potent alliterative punch of "paving paradise and putting up a parking lot," which is a kind of shorthand to what is happening in a society where capitalism has run amok. Deforestation equals more parking lots, which equals more cars, which equals more pollution, and Joni's lyrics succinctly foresaw the environmental problems that have only been exacerbated since she wrote the song. The notion that we'd need a tree museum because we might endanger the life of trees, so crucial to providing us oxygen to breathe, seems like science fiction, until we look at the science of dendrochronology or witness the dead ironwood trees in Senegal, West Africa, where rainfall has dropped 20% to 30% in the twentieth and twenty-first centuries. Perhaps the greatest irony in "Big Yellow Taxi" is that the very forces that have helped decimate the environment are the same forces that will stand to gain by charging an admission fee for us to experience our human birthright. And the claw of this change reaches out from the trees to pinch the human body—when our crops are pumped with pesticides and genetically modified, the end result will be greater disease and even diminished sexual energy, all in the name of profit. "Give me spots on my apples," Joni beseeches, "But leave me the birds and the bees / Please!"

"Big Yellow Taxi" has been covered by everyone from Bob Dylan to the Counting Crows, and reached the top twenty on the charts in her native Canada. The song has been sampled by Janet Jackson and Q-Tip, and there has even been a jazz version recorded. The sheer fact that it lives on, forty-odd years after it was first recorded, is testament to its sustained power. I write this homage on the very day that Barack Obama, a president for whom I campaigned and voted with great hope, has once again conceded to his Republican counterparts, who argue that corporations are people, by backing off from having stricter smog standards—a U.S. Environmental Protection Agency-backed initiative that many environmentalists and scientists see as crucial to human and environmental health. Yet not important enough, apparently, in the face of special interests to defend, even by our staunchly Democratic president.

The big yellow taxi of capitalism is careening wildly out of control, and now more than ever we need someone like the courageous Joni Mitchell to remind us what should be obvious: that our most important resources are our natural world and each other, in no particular order; for without one, we couldn't have the other. I, for one, don't want the headlong horsepower rush any longer. Hit the brakes, taxi and flip the meter back. Veer curbside and cut out the exhaust. You've got one less fare to take, because this brother is getting off and walking.

WOODSTOCK

I came upon a child of God
He was walking along the road
And I asked him, "Where are you going?"
And this he told me—he said,
"I'm going on down to Yasgur's farm
I'm going to join a rock 'n' roll band
I'm going to camp out on the land
I'm going to try an' get my soul free!"
He said
"We are stardust
We are golden
And we've got to get ourselves
Back to the garden!"

"Then can I walk beside you
I have come here to lose the smog
And I feel
To be
A cog
In something turning
Well, maybe it is just the time of year
Or maybe it's the time of man
I don't know who I am
But life is for learning"

He said
"We are stardust
We are golden
And we've got to get ourselves
Back to the garden!"

By the time we got to Woodstock
We were half a million strong
And everywhere you looked
There was song and celebration
And I dreamed I saw the bombers
Riding shotgun in the sky
And they were turning into butterflies
Above our nation

We are stardust
Come from billion year old carbon
We are golden
Caught up in some devil's bargain
And we've got to get ourselves
Back to the garden

STARDUST IN THE GARDEN: ON THE OPPOSITIONAL POETRY OF "WOODSTOCK"

JON ANDERSEN

I prefer Mitchell's haunting performance of her song-poem "Woodstock" to the jubilant bounce of Crosby, Stills, Nash and Young's version; her deliberately paced voice soars like an angel or a bomber. In her performance, the lyrics achieve altitude and resonance—tinged with ominous risk.

A quick survey of the basic facts of "Woodstock" suggests that it could easily be dismissed as a period piece. As the title indicates, the song was inspired by that specific, iconic three-day festival of love, peace and music in 1969, the Woodstock Music and Art Fair. We are told that during this festival a whole generation carved—with song, dance, lovemaking and drugs—a new paradisal space into the nation that Martin Luther King, Jr. had, only two years earlier, called the "greatest purveyor of violence in the world."

All you have to do, though, is rub this mythic veneer with your thumb to see the reality beneath. For starters, it wasn't a whole generation. My father, for example, was just back from Vietnam, looking to put the world back together by finding honest work and wooing my mother at her parent's short-haired working-class bar. And the predominantly white and privileged party in the Catskill Mountains was a half a day's drive and a whole world away from places like Harlem.

Still, I believe Joni Mitchell's "Woodstock" persists and insists. Powerfully. Reading or listening to the lyrics, I am tempted to say the song transcends. But nothing really transcends—things go on or they don't. No art or utterance exists without some kind of historical or social limitation. Instead, "Woodstock" might achieve what the Uruguayan writer Eduardo Galeano suggested that the very best art can hope to achieve: merely help to aid in social change—to encourage transformation. Forget about transcendence: today, "Woodstock" remains a soundtrack for personal engagement in the world.

Listening closely to "Woodstock," we have the feeling we are really going places, not just along for the ride to Yasgur's Farm, but pushed and pulled through a searching pattern of oppositions. The song gains momentum through stunning imagistic foils of the ethereal and sidereal on one hand, and the gritty and corporeal on the other: "We are stardust / Come from billion year old carbon / We are golden" creates a luminous backdrop for the young man ("a child of God") who, looking to "lose the smog," declares: "'I'm going on down to Yasgur's Farm / I'm going to join a rock 'n' roll band / I'm going to camp out on the land / I'm going to try an' get my soul free!'" (For an unlikely comparison, but one that suggests the literary achievement of "Woodstock," I'd like to note that the set up of an oppositional pattern between heavenly and earthly imagery was a favorite technique of Thomas Hardy in his poetry and prose. His *Tess of the D'Urbervilles*, for example, struggles through a life of relentless labor and bodily trauma, always under skies of luminous stars, sublime morning light or otherworldly darkness.)

The second major oppositional pattern in "Woodstock" emerges between the return and the journey forward: Mitchell makes brilliant use of the Christian concept of returning to a prelapsarian state: "We've got to get ourselves / Back to the garden!" Imagining Eden has the same literary purpose as imagining Utopia—the endless struggle for perfection does not lead to perfection for the characters or for readers, but the only alternative is stasis, death, of not having a story to tell at all. To imagine a paradise in our past or in our future trains our imaginations to go big, go long, go beyond the provincial. If we are engaged readers and listeners, we'll even go so far as to move beyond the literary altogether, back toward the real human world and forward toward the world we might have a hand in creating. In the journey in "Woodstock," a collective "half a million strong" tries to get "back to the Garden," while "Caught up in some devil's bargain." They do it together. Yes, in the real life event (not the song), they were largely limited by the exclusions of race and class I mention above, but we all are. The mainstream mystification of Woodstock and the '60s aside, we owe many of those kids kudos for pushing back against such exclusions.

The crucial effect of these oppositional patterns is not to be stuck in their tension or trapped in nostalgia for what was—or for what memory has tricked us into believing was. (For my generation, too, and the generations coming along, there is the danger of vicarious nostalgia—the rabbit hole of "Oh, I was born too late....") As of 2011, the breathtaking altitude, celebratory resonance and ominous risk of "Woodstock" are, tonally, just right. Right now, the Occupy movement has been globalized, calling out the lies of finance capitalism. The Woodstock Festival itself now seems prelapsarian: long before the Towers fell, before we fell into this state of Endless War, before torture became an official practice and patriotic duty. As it turns out, the whole postmodern promise of the "end of history" was a deadly ruse, a devil's bargain in which we stopped being workers and fathers and mothers and citizens and lovers so that we could become employees and consumers. In exchange, just enough of us were served a little piece of the apple pie.

The other night, my wife Denise and I found ourselves standing outside our old farmhouse under a starry sky. Our ten-year-old son, Kit, slept in his warm room, which only recently belonged to his older brother, Miles, now at college. I had just hand-sown a cover crop of rye on our big vegetable garden that day. I am not religious, but, looking at the stars strewn like seeds across the blackness, I felt that I vaguely understood why people believe in God. For a moment, it was even possible to believe that this was paradise.

But that invitation to relax, to feel satisfied, is spun with a serpent tongue. I noticed that one of the stars moved smoothly, arcing high above us—not a star, but a passenger jet. Somewhere, not a star, not a passenger jet, but a bomber or a drone moved high above another nation, across another family's sky. Here in our own country, millions of children lay awake, hungry.

No, this is not the Garden, and our souls are not yet free. We'll just have to do the best we can: teach, organize, write, join a local protest. It won't be sufficient. Imagining a time of true freedom, though—where all people, not just my family and I, have enough to live on and can do that living joyfully, without the fear of war, a time when we have replaced those bombers and drones with butterflies—keeps us moving purposefully, each taking up our small and crucial roles in the grand narrative. We need more songs and poems like Joni Mitchell's "Woodstock," asking us to stretch our notions of what can be, encouraging us to be part of this collective journey, never quite arriving, perhaps, but always a little farther down the road.

I AM STARDUST

SUSAN DEER CLOUD

I grew up in an extended family of storytellers and artistic and musical people. I realized before I was forced to go to kindergarten that I was a weaver of stories and poems. By the time 1969 arrived, I also realized that for me to fully embody my creative gifts I was going to have to be fierce, brave and resilient. By 1969 I had already run away from college twice to live for some months in Washington, DC—an education in itself—and briefly in western Massachusetts in the woods. In DC, while my drafted eldest brother was in Vietnam, I participated in anti-war marches and marches for civil and other rights. In the woods, I communed with the ghost of Thoreau. Although I am not one to debunk the idealism of the '60s decade, which was real and beautiful, I can recall clearly some of the meanness of the era that tied in with the Vietnam War, racism, sexism and hatred of "the other" altogether. One of my most vivid memories is of a crew-cut, gray-haired man kicking his tail-wagging white puppy in its ribs for prancing up to me and licking my fingers on Liberty, New York, Main Street. "Get away from that dirty hippie!" he yelled. I have a collection of similar anecdotes.

Dirty hippie. Young women like myself were viewed as sexually loose "hippies" or "flower children," and soon we became hip to those males predators who used "free love" as a tool to get fast food McSex with no responsibility attached to the human beings they were preying on. Those were days of liberation, including the inception of the feminist movement of the 1970s. Girls and women were fed up with double standards and being oppressed and discriminated against. And there I was—female, Indian, poor, beyond the north end of Appalachia—learning about the ways the patriarchal, capitalist "system" conspired against the free spirit and ecstatic body I was born with. People have long spoken of "angry young men," whereas I was an "angry young woman" with an irrepressible streak of underlying sweetness. Yes, I was one of those flower children who danced around flashing the peace symbol and lilting "Peace! Love!" After all, the hippies' ideals were generally close to my Native ways and beliefs.

So when I returned home from my wanderings in the summer of 1969 and heard about what was "going down" on Yasgur's farm in Bethel, NY, I imagined that we dreamers were headed for an embodiment of that communal peace so many of us were yearning for. The festival was about a twenty minute drive from where my family lived in Livingston Manor. Not only that, I am descended from a Mohawk medicine woman and Bethel is even closer to where my ancestress lived and healed people in nineteenth-century Mongaup Creek Valley. My Iroquois ancestors highly influenced the first white feminists who gathered at Seneca Falls, and now braless and fearless young women in vivid ankle-length dresses and Indian beads were heading for a farm field in the Catskill foothills. I, of course, wanted to join them, but my mother tightened her lips into tomahawk blades and said, "If you go over there, you can't stay in our house anymore. I'll throw you out on the street." We fought about it, but she refused to relent. Come "garbage day," I was searching for one of the long dresses that my Great Aunt Ida had sewn for me and I could not find it or other long dresses. Then I remembered the early morning brake squeals of the garbage truck. I asked my mother, "You didn't throw out my long dresses, did you?" Increased tightening of her lips, and this time no battle words, only silence. I had received my answer.

Forever sadly, I didn't make it to the Woodstock Festival and listen day and night to music and glisten like a wildflower in the rain and mud and go skinny-dipping with the other flower children and do whatever it was my mother feared I might do. I stayed home and secretly cried in my room and more than ever before longed to run away from the "town without pity."

Decades later, driving back from giving a poetry reading and listening to the FM radio on one of those lonely highway night drives, an interview with Joni Mitchell streamed through my speakers. The singer/writer/artist was talking about why she had not performed at the Woodstock Festival, about her song "Woodstock" not arising from her being there in body because her agent had scheduled her for The Dick Cavett Show that Tuesday. Hearing her speak about her absence at the festival unexpectedly brought balm to the wound of my not being allowed to take part in that historical gathering of "half a million strong." My Woodstock had been bitter tears in a hot, stuffy, upstairs bedroom. The bitterness was not only about my mother's refusal to let me go such a short distance to that magnificent psychedelic gathering, but for what America had done to my mother—making her afraid to express her Indian-ness and her desires to fly free as I loved to fly free. She used to say to me, "You live out my dreams, for I cannot," but on the other hand she grew fearful when those dreams burst exuberantly and defiantly past small town boundaries and smaller minds. My mother was of a generation of Northeast Indians who lay low and did nothing to cause the word "savage" to be flung at their attempted invisibility.

Circling back to Joni Mitchell's song "Woodstock," I have lived with it for well over three decades; often I play it when I make one of my journeys back to the Catskill Mountains, where I've not lived since I was a young woman. I play it when I drive to the Woodstock Festival site to walk barefooted in the soft, grassy field of tie-dyed ghosts or to show an out-of-state friend this historical place where smiling strangers still gather together in peace. In a sense, "Woodstock" is my "going home" song, an assuaging of the constant undertow of homesickness that I feel not only for the mountains but for my Turtle Island that long ago was invaded, raped, wounded and stolen.

Joni Mitchell's "Woodstock" is brilliantly rooted in the mystical tradition of Judeo-Christianity and other worthy spiritual traditions, as well. The song works as a sophisticated poem that glimmers with rich and evocative images, allusions, chants and rhymes that are often interior and slant (no dull, end rhyme, pop song treacle here). The singer's handling of pronouns in the song weaves the "I" and the "we" together in a silken fashion that contributes to the song's moving from the individual "I" to the communal "we." From the opening lines, "I came upon a child of God / He was walking along the road" to the final two lines, "And we've got to get ourselves / Back to the garden," the words soar phoenix-like into profound archetypal realities. The song establishes how any stranger can be "a child of God" on a journey back to the Garden, to the paradise of innocence, before falling into "some devil's bargain" that has turned people into cogs and shadowed the sky with bombers riding "shotgun."

For me, as an indigenous Catskill woman, "Woodstock" expresses the heart of my tradition. The "child of God" whom the I-narrator meets on the road tells her of his returning to the land, music and freedom, followed by the refrain:

We are stardust
We are golden
And we've got to get ourselves
Back to the garden!

This song is suffused with refrain and chant-like attributes, chant being an ancient device for expressing mourning as well as joy and ecstasy. "Woodstock" pivots delicately on both, on that haunting sense and sound tied in with greed, war and a world turned coldly mechanical, while simultaneously dreaming a return to land and Garden. How moving when the I-narrator sings to the child of God, "'Then can I walk beside you / I have come here to lose the smog.'" The smog itself, in this context, can be regarded not only as pollution of air but pollution of the human spirit.

Beaded throughout "Woodstock" are references to the cosmos, and in the crescendo of the final stanza Joni Mitchell's song soars into poetic transcendence where the I-narrator dreamed she saw the bombers "turning into butterflies / Above our nation," where she repeats that "we are stardust" then adds we come from "billion year old carbon." We humans and all life on earth: carbon-based related and stardust-interconnected. As delicate/strong as the poetry of the song is, one cannot feel its full effect without hearing it sung by the writer herself. The voice Mitchell brings to her song is what my people would call a medicine woman's voice, the Peacemaker's voice—powerfully soft and dignified. It is not junkyard dog weak, aggressive and loud. Both her voice and the piano-playing at times touch on minor notes that are haunting, an undercurrent that locks into "the devil's bargain" that entices us to settle for the non-life of the cog in the smog and endless war. How ingeniously wonderful that after the song's lyrics Joni Mitchell ends it with no words at all, only exquisite, enchanting, haunting sounds trailing off into a sky of quiet. She leaves us with that gentle urging of the final lines and a loveliness of sound beyond our human language that too often divides us from each other.

"Woodstock" is as profoundly about love as any song can be; not about any "free love" as tied in with 1960s "sexual revolution," but with an ancient, tender, alchemical love reminding us that "we are golden." In the years before my mother died of breast cancer, she apologized to me for being "too strict" and not allowing me to be a part of Woodstock Nation. In 1977 she warned, "We are losing more and more of our freedoms, and the ones being born now won't even know what freedoms they are missing," and added that she now understood how I felt when I was that young, anti-war flower child embarking on her poet's journey.

Blue-eyed Joni Mitchell of the high, startling cheekbones, I came across a child of God one day (I say Great Mystery). And that child turned out to be you, northern sister of Sami lineage, who unbeknownst to herself allowed me to walk beside her on the road. Thank you, nia:wen, Joni, for keeping me company all those lonely times I've driven back to what I call my "heart country"—to the Catskills, to Bethel—still "going to camp out on the land" to "get my soul free." As for the ones who have been born to fewer and fewer freedoms, many of them tell me they like your "Woodstock" song and wish to be on that road, too.

THE CIRCLE GAME

Yesterday a child came out to wonder
Caught a dragonfly inside a jar
Fearful when the sky was full of thunder
And tearful at the falling of a star
And the seasons—they go round and round
And the painted ponies go up and down
We're captive on the carousel of time
We can't return
We can only look behind
From where we came
And go round and round and round
In the circle game

Then the child moved ten times round the seasons
Skated over ten clear frozen streams
Words like when you're older must appease him
And promises of someday make his dreams
And the seasons—they go round and round
And the painted ponies go up and down
We're captive on the carousel of time
We can't return
We can only look behind
From where we came
And go round and round and round
In the circle game

Sixteen springs and sixteen summers gone now...
Cartwheels turn to car wheels thru the town
And they tell him take your time it won't be long now
Till you drag your feet to slow the circles down
And the seasons—they go round and round
And the painted ponies go up and down

We're captive on the carousel of time
We can't return
We can only look behind
From where we came
And go round and round and round
In the circle game

So the years spin by and now the boy is twenty
Though his dreams have lost some grandeur coming true
There'll be new dreams—maybe better dreams, and plenty
Before the last revolving year is through
The seasons—they go round and round
And the painted ponies go up and down
We're captive on the carousel of time
We can't return
We can only look behind
From where we came
And go round and round and round
In the circle game

ROUND AND ROUND

KRISTIN ROUND GROVES

My father set out to chronicle our lives—mine, my sisters' and my brother's—on video cassette.

We lived in front of scorching spotlights clipped to behemoth video cameras perched on my dad's shoulder.

We were:

pre-Facebook;

pre-Internet;

pre-Eminem;

pre-Nirvana;

thankfully pre-Bobby Brown and Whitney and Z-Cavaricci...

Just about Sesame Street and the Muppet's era when he was at the peak of his videography career.

The movie quality was passable.

The pictures were grainy—especially Beta and Super-8s—and often jumped, but at least were viewable. Nowadays, video like that is even emulated for that vintage feel.

The sound was awful.

All you could hear was whoosh! bang! bumpbump! on the microphone, as if every day were a hurricane and not just a summer breeze. Because of this, my dad had the undeniable privilege of setting all of our old home videos to music.

The music of choice for my father was Dylan, Jethro Tull, Boston, CSN+/-Y, Fleetwood Mac (I know I'm leaving many out) and Joni.

Always Joni.

If it were only up to my Dad, I think it would be nothing but Joni. He loved her voice and her words. Her poetry.

I digress.

I remember a few of the movies distinctly, even though many years have passed since I've watched them. One that I remember best is set to "The Circle Game."

"Yesterday a child came out to wonder"

It's my dad's college reunion: 1979, less than ten years out. It takes place in August at a Rhode Island state park. The stone outdoor grill is going with hot dogs and burgers over charcoal. Cheap beer flows freely. The standard dress for men appears to be: very short shorts, with or without a longitudinal white stripe down each side; tight, v-necked, collared T-shirts; tube socks; running shoes; a choice between gold chains and slicked back hair or no jewelry, longish hair, mustache and beard. The game of choice is used-to-be-an-athlete volleyball. I've played this myself before, so don't take that the wrong way. That's just what it is.

The camera pans off to a different scene from the same reunion. A few of the new moms and wives are sitting on a plaid picnic blanket under a perfect, cloud-speckled, blue sky. They have hair that used to be long and beautiful, parted down the middle, but recently was chopped off or slung into a ponytail to become more conducive to motherhood. They wear cotton T-shirts and shorts or jeans. They are laughing and happy, watching the men make fools of themselves or the babies trying to take their first steps.

And this is what always got me…

My dad spliced the whole picnic video to the sound of "The Circle Game." It was timed perfectly. The child caught dragonflies, moved ten times round the seasons, turned cartwheels into car wheels and started dreaming new dreams, when suddenly there was a burst of applause.

As a typical, egotistical child, it always seemed that the applause was for me. It came just as I (a chubby ten-month-old) toddled clumsily off of the picnic blanket, into the green grass, toward my mother. And the scene, and song, ended…

Years have passed and now I am thirty-three.

I have watched three of my children take their own first steps and receive their own applause. I now watch my youngest daughter's fascination with a stinkbug as it stilts across the floor in front of her. It will be her catching dragonflies soon.

I see my oldest son becoming a playground mediator—easing hurts, establishing a playground code of ethics and being looked to as a leader. He then comes home to hear "when you're older," as he asks to watch a PG-13 movie.

I watch my middle daughter pore over books for hours on end, oblivious to anything in the world around her, and realize that there are not enough years left between her and a steering wheel. Watch out world…

My son says squirrels will go extinct soon because of reckless drivers.

My daughter says she wasn't paying attention to me because her brain kept her busy "thinking about lions AND tigers, mommy."

When I look at my present, and meld it with the beautifully choreographed videography in my minds past, I see more clearly. My dreams have, indeed, lost a lot of grandeur coming true. But in my children there will be new dreams, maybe better dreams, certainly plenty of new dreams, before the last revolving year is thru.

Thank you, Joni.

UP AND DOWN

JOHN SORNBERGER

It's 1969, man, and I'm twenty. I've got long hair, two tickets to some huge outdoor concert in upstate N.Y. and it could be another Summer of Love. But I can't groove. Sugar Mountain is nowhere in sight for me, not even in the rearview mirror. I'm prime meat for the draft, can't concentrate, can't get easy with myself. That's a drag. And then there's the music. It's all around. New sounds every day, and everybody I know is really into it. But I'm not feeling it… I can't, because the music doesn't get inside when I'm uptight in my throat, chest and belly. And that's most of the time these days. So I've pretty much stopped trying to listen. It's kind of lonely…

But wait… it's right now again and I'm sixty-three. I've moved forty-three times round the seasons since then and, like Joni says, I can't go back. I'm glad about that but, as I look back, I realize why "The Circle Game" was so important to me then and why it still is.

"The Circle Game" reminds me of where I've come, that I am more easy with myself now, and that today I can enjoy my life more fully. "The Circle Game" was one of precious few songs that I was able to listen to, feel and enjoy in the '60s and '70s. Somehow it got through my anxiety and depression, made me feel good top to bottom, right in my midline. Still does. That surprises me and makes me very curious. How, after forty years, can listening to or even just reading the words still evoke such a positive and visceral response?

After investigating, I've found out that it is not nostalgia or wanting to be young on Sugar Mountain or anything like that. There is, rather, something about the words themselves that evokes my feelings and my appreciation. I find that Joni's words prompt me to actively listen in a way that leads to both cognitive and felt understanding of their meaning. It is a process of active or participatory listening, and it has three distinct but interdependent and repeating steps. I've discovered that the process immediately activates when I hear or begin reading the very first group of words. Here is how it works:

STEP 1:

I listen to or read the first lines or group of words and they are instantly made sense of

STEP 2:

by transforming the auditory input into remembered or imagined images, which, in turn, trigger feelings in my midline.

STEP 3:

When the evoked images and feelings are consistent with my beliefs, life experience and what I want to experience, I am motivated to circle back.

STEP 1:

I listen even more closely to the next group of words and then go to

STEP 2:

Where I select one remembered or imagined image that interests me and pay very close attention to it. I make it clear, bright, in color and large enough to step into. Then, I engage all of my senses in that time and place. I do this long enough to access a powerful feeling representative of that remembered or imagined experience and to make cognitive evaluations that I will use in the next step.

STEP 3:

When this evoked image and feeling is consistent with my beliefs, life experience and what I want to experience in this moment in time, I am motivated to circle back.

STEP 1:

Then I listen closely to the next group of image producing words… And round and round I go through this repeating process of hearing, seeing, feeling and evaluating until the song or poem ends.

At this point, I'd like to share a few examples of this participatory listening process in action when I hear or read the poetic words of "The Circle Game."

STEP 1:

"Yesterday a child came out to wonder
Caught a dragonfly inside a jar"

STEP 2:

This word group first transformed into imagined images of catching a dragonfly inside a jar (something I had never actually done). Then, right away, an actual memory appeared of catching a firefly inside a jar on a clear summer night in my best friend's field. When I chose this image to step into, I felt once again like a child of wonder. I remember what that was like, especially as I hold the jar up to the dark, starry sky and watch as my very own star blinks on and off and on.

STEP 3:

Joni's words evoked a memory and powerful feeling linked with it and provided me with motivation to continue listening to find out what I would be prompted to see and feel next.

STEP 1:

"Then the child moved ten times round the seasons
Skated over ten clear frozen streams"

(It happens that I grew up in the country, and there was a shallow stream down in the far corner of the property. There was a span of about ten years when, starting in early winter, as often as we could my best friend and I would sled down to the stream and test the ice until it would hold up. When it did, we would skate or slide on our boots for hours at a time. There was much laughter and teasing, especially when one of us broke through).

STEP 2:

Stepping into any of the remembered images from that ten-year span recaptures a strong feeling of adventure and freedom.

STEP 3:

This is powerful feeling, and one that motivates me to continue listening to find out what I will be prompted to see and feel next.

STEP 1:

"And the seasons—they go round and round
And the painted ponies go up and down"

STEP 2:

These words evoke vivid, moving images of painted ponies on a carousel going up and down as they go round and round. I'm not sure if these images are remembered, imagined or a little of both, but they are in vivid color, they are moving and they are beautiful. I definitely enjoy stepping into them.

STEP 3:

I experience feelings of appreciation and awe and, once again, I am deeply motivated to listen closely to what comes next... And round and round I go through this process of hearing, seeing, feeling and evaluating until the song ends.

It's clear that I love many of the images and feelings that "The Circle Game" evokes, but Joni's words do not just evoke images and feelings I cherish. Nor should they, if the message and the observations she is making about growing up are to ring true. In fact, there are words in "Circle Game" that, as I listen, evoke memories and feelings of loss, disappointment, fear and sadness as well.

These feelings are sobering, but not overwhelming, and, for me, they lend credibility to the message of hope Joni is so artfully conveying. "There'll be new dreams—maybe better dreams, and plenty." Thank you, Joni.

ALL I WANT

I am on a lonely road and I am traveling
Traveling
Traveling
Traveling
Looking for something
What can it be?
Oh I hate you some
I hate you some
I love you some
I love you when I forget about me
I want to be strong
I want to laugh along
I want to belong to the living
Alive
Alive
I want to get up and jive
I want to wreck my stockings in some juke box dive
Do you want
Do you want
Do you want to dance with me baby?
Do you want to take a chance
On maybe finding some sweet romance with me baby?
Well, come on!

All I really really want our love to do
Is to bring out the best in me
And in you too
All I really really want our love to do
Is to bring out the best in me
And in you
I want to talk to you
I want to shampoo you
I want to renew you again and again

Applause
Applause
Life is our cause
When I think of your kisses
My mind see-saws
Do you see
Do you see
Do you see how you hurt me baby?
So I hurt you too
Then we both get
So blue

I am on a lonely road and I am traveling
Looking for the key to set me free
Oh the jealousy
The greed is the unraveling
It's the unraveling
And it undoes all the joy that could be
I want to have fun
I want to shine like the sun
I want to be the one that you want to see
I want to knit you a sweater
Want to write you a love letter
I want to make you feel better
I want to make you feel free
I want to make you feel free
Could we love
And still feel free?

ALL I WANT

ALEXANDER MACK

In a quiet car rolling across the thick, hushed night. At the beckoning of Father who fiddles with an iPod, I readily OPEN my auditory receptors—(wide)—to the thick, thick silence. Waiting.

Instantly: bright, sharp, syncopated pluckings begin to bubble out of a buzzing drone, and a thumpTHUMP like the bass drum of a Latin jazz chart. All leading to... something—on the verge. Then, "I am on a lonely road aand I am traavelling-trAvelling-trAvelling-trAvelling." I am swimming in a velvet voice. A rose-colored, liquid voice—a wet paint voice, because it is that smooth and rich. And she is singing right to me, but it's more than that—is she singing into me? This voice speaks so very much inside of me that it may even be my own, though transfigured: into some wet, rose-colored womanly perfection of gorgeous paint.

And her words: she has gathered up the fragmented thoughts and emotions that have squirmed around my brain for the past few months—or perhaps all my life?—(most of them incomprehensible to me) and mashed them into a cohesive monologue. And here it is: the final product, sung to me now so sweetly.

> All I really really want our love to do
> Is to bring out the best in me
> And in you
> I want to talk to you
> I wanna shampoo you
> I want to renew you again and again

And this is why I find myself feeling more and more that her voice is in fact... mine; she isn't just singing the English translation of that indescribable love that lives in my spirit: she is that love. In this moment, this sacred marriage of language and melody, she has become the experience of that love itself. She knows me. She knows humans: she sees how our love causes us to make each other suffer. She feels it all and she can paint a picture of it—with her poetry and with her soaring voice.

> Do you see
> Do you see
> Do you see how you hurt me, baby?
> So I hurt you too
> Then we both get
> So blue

She knows me, because most days my soul is an instrumental, with no clarity, no words with which to process reality, only raw and seemingly senseless feeling. She finds those hidden words—the ones that can somehow capture and translate that unintelligible emotional fabric I seem to share with her (and perhaps with the rest of mankind). The velvet rose of her spirit stands naked before my mind—dancing, shimmering, singing—and I see that it is also my spirit.... And how strange and how beautiful that someone could throw off all veils and disguises and speak into you with her bare soul until the very honesty of her exposed inner monologue wipes the dust from your mirror and makes clearer your own reflection. And what a revelation to find that your own reflection is not only yours but...

> I want to knit you a sweater
> Want to write you a love letter
> I want to make you feel better
> I want to make you feel free

As her voice paints these unashamed desires in my ears in the wildest, wettest shades of orange, rose, pale yellow, violet, the thought floats to my consciousness that I probably would have fallen in love with Joni Mitchell had I been more than just a biological possibility in the '60s.

I heard soon after discovering her music that Joni was a painter as well as a musician, so I found it peculiar that "All I Want" and the rest of *Blue* had sent me manically applying oil pastel to some paper I had lying around. "River" produced a rainbow-colored tree heavy with sorrowful love on a hill of shivering grass, which I gave to my girlfriend at the time. I didn't know it four years ago when I first immersed myself in that album, but *Blue* was a major spark that began to transform the way I approach writing music. Every aspect of how Mitchell's music and words were composed seemed to actually mirror the process of painting in a certain unexplainable way. Her songs gave me especially vivid visual impressions, and I soon began noticing a really important bond between the auditory and the visual in my own creative process. Today, I don't believe I could ever separate the act of writing music from the inspiration I find in visual art and the visual world. Each shapes the other mysteriously and intimately. Just thinking of this fills me with intense gratitude for Joni Mitchell, a woman who has been brave enough to erase the imaginary lines between art forms. For decades the world has watched her shamelessly explore herself and her creative process without lines or boxes or boundaries, and I cannot think of anything more honorable and beautiful to see an artist do. All of us who continue to create and explore the boundaries of art are indebted to her, whether we know it or not.

ALL I WANT

KATHLEEN McELROY

Joni. Pick a song, one song. And I keep coming up with a string of phrases and melodies from the album *Blue*. I found *Blue* when I was trying to sort out what it meant to be a woman. Joni Mitchell was one of the voices that cried for me in the wilderness. It was the '70s, I was in my late teens, change was careening around me. We had already burned our bras and the birth control pill promised a chance at true freedom. The war was finally ending. I was lost and not a soul, not even me, knew it.

I was raised Catholic. I was raised to be a teacher so if my husband died I would have a career to fall back on. And while my mother was basically a gentle woman, she was never a happy woman. I don't know why. And she was not one to share intimacies. So here I was, a young woman torn between my beloved childhood *Lives of the Saints* and the promise of Wild Love. I was afraid to break out and afraid to stay in. I was pigheaded and in rebellion, with no confidence, seemingly no common sense, no desire to be a teacher and too frightened to shout out loud (although I hid that well behind weekend drinking). I was clueless about love and frightened by the power of sex. I was looking for a direction, for a persona, for something different from the person I was raised to be. I was repressed, guilt-ridden, anxiety-prone and a teenager. I was not as smart as I appeared to be, I was so much angrier than I knew and I was incapable, at the time, of deep attachment.

And there was Joni Mitchell and *Blue*. That album was a revelation for me. Somehow, Joni had words that did more than simply illuminate that era. Her poetry, in all its intimacy, covered the broad landscape that was my life. Her lyrics were poetry of change in the internal landscape. In the album's songs lay paths through the labyrinth. She sang about love—complicated and sometimes unrequited, unconnected, impermanent. She understood that it was so easy to make mistakes. She understood the pain. But most of all, she made me feel that it was okay to want to be alive, to feel, to have fun. Her words allowed me to embrace my need for freedom, my quest for my own adventure.

I was on a lonely road and I was travelling...

The themes of love and freedom and place in society are timeless. Wars rage. Political egos shatter lives. Concepts and ideals alter and sometimes change. At day's end, I think it is, in part, the artist's ability to effectively and imaginatively mirror the times she lives in that leaves the enduring mark. It is also precisely that gift which makes an artist well loved and popular in her own time.

In "All I Want," Joni managed to mirror my confusion and exuberance about love. It spoke of all the things I yearned for: freedom, joy, great sex and unconditional love. It acknowledged the dark side that can creep in and twist love: those ancient demons of jealousy and greed. It spoke of love in all its simplicity and in all its complexity. It gave me a benchmark of true love that I hold to still. Any writer knows how difficult it is to accomplish those feats.

"All I Want" celebrated an abundant enthusiasm, an embrace of the joy and energy and possibilities inherent in being alive with all the zest and passion of a gypsy queen or a female Zorba the Greek: "Alive, alive, I want to get up and jive/ I want to wreck my stockings in some jukebox dive" It made me want to dance, my skirts swirling in the moonlight.

Today, it remains one of my favorite Joni songs. Those lyrics—"I am on a lonely road and I am traveling / Traveling / Traveling / Traveling"—pass through my mind whenever I hit a rough spot on Life's Existential Road. As a poet, they allow me to step back and validate my instincts. They help me to reach deep and go for the intimacy of the moment. And my definition of true love remains in these lines: "All I really really want our love to do / Is to bring out the best in me / And in you too." If I'm angling for something other than that, it's not really coming from a place of true love. Thank you, Joni.

CAREY

The wind is in from Africa
Last night I couldn't sleep
Oh, you know it sure is hard to leave here Carey
But it's really not my home
My fingernails are filthy
I've got beach tar on my feet
And I miss my clean white linen
And my fancy French cologne
Oh Carey get out your cane
And I'll put on some silver
Oh you're a mean old Daddy
But I like you fine

Come on down to the Mermaid Café
And I will
Buy you a bottle of wine
And we'll laugh
And toast to nothing
And smash our empty glasses down
Let's have a round for these freaks and these soldiers
A round for these friends of mine
Let's have another round
For the bright red devil
Who keeps me in this tourist town
Come on Carey get out your cane
And I'll put on some silver
Oh you're a mean old Daddy
But I like you fine

Maybe I'll go to Amsterdam
Maybe I'll go to Rome
And rent me a grand piano
And put some flowers 'round my room
But let's not talk about fare-thee-wells now
The night is a starry dome
And they're playin' that scratchy rock and roll
Beneath the Matala Moon
Come on Carey get out your cane
I'll put on some silver
We'll go to the Mermaid Café
Have fun tonight

The wind is in from Africa
Last night I couldn't sleep
Oh you know it sure is hard to leave here
But it's really not my home
Maybe it's been too long a time
Since I was scramblin' down in the street
Now they got me used to that clean white linen
And that fancy French cologne
Oh Carey get out your cane
I'll put on my finest silver
We'll go to the Mermaid Café
Have fun tonight

CAREY

LOUISE B. HALFE (SKY DANCER)

THE CREE WANDERER

I am busy swallowing this blistered
body that moves
Like the slithering wind.
For the moment I've paused
In this shallow pit where water
Once existed
To reflect
And to fill my mouth with what
The heart has eaten.

Darkness measured the days'
Teachings and
Lightning swaddled life as if a child
lifted her folded eyelid. A flood of light
lit and kicked the pulsing earth.

I watched the earth roll, and come to a stop.
With a willow switch I urged her on.
She labored inch by inch until she gave
Birth. A turtle left her womb.
A second birth left the earth.

First Turtle held the second
Ripped her belly and released
The rivers.
A shadow stood in the pit and handed
An arrowhead to me. For three
thousand years it lay asleep, waiting

For this light.
I held her gently
Against my heart where it suckled
On my skin and breast.

When the dark sun
Was swallowed, Chief Thunder
hollered, and roared
With my ancestors following.
Raindrop women came carrying
swift little lakes that fell into the our
Robbing mouths.

Over trees, hills and prairie flat
The songs of wind, beast and child
Stitched and laced the young,
Old and wild.

This lament I share with you
Giving Creation a difficult time
Digging from the belly's pit
You've left us with your songs.

I've listened repeatedly to two of Joni's CDs and it wasn't so much a particular song,
but phrases here and there, and her voice.
Joni's voice is never stagnant; it rolls over prairie hills, laughs and cries with the coyotes.
She shares a story into the night with the voice of the owl
her eyes boring into the spirit
The words mean to drill and be heard.
Every phrase connects the mind and travels directly
To the heart. She is a miner, deep in someone's cave, probing and investigating.
Of course she is a poem herself, an art magician in song and flesh.
I travelled on the skirts of the poetic song
and the singer invited me to wrestle with the wind.

FOR JONI

I've put Joni on the road
Spinning on my computer program
She bends loaded down
With her backpack
Checking her tires
She lies on the pavement
Receiving from the universe
I love her "Carey"
Singing bird-like
"California" rolling into my life
What can I say?
She sings me into
This life.

CAREY

MAUREEN CROTEAU

I finally understand my Aunt Sis. In her last years she would struggle when a doctor asked how old she was.

"Forty-five?" she would say, looking at me for help.

"Actually, Sis, you're ninety."

"Ninety?" She would ponder that for a moment. "That doesn't seem possible, does it?"

"No," I would say. "Not to me."

In the 1950s, Sis was the image of the well-dressed, forty-something career woman—stiletto heels, earrings that matched her necklaces, lipstick that came from a department store. When she really dressed up, she wore midnight blue mascara. It was enough to make a young girl's heart ache with envy and pride.

She was fun.

As I sat with her in countless doctors' offices fifty years later, I thought that I understood why the question of age stumped her. Neurons. Synapses. Blood sugar. Oxygen.

I did not understand at all. What I know now—as I am older and becoming older still—is that she was right about her age. Forty-five was a good age for her, so she stopped there. That is what we all do. Our bodies go along from day to day, aging according to their own schedules, and that is nothing but a surprise to the person we are inside. We look at a calendar. We look in a mirror. We awaken one morning and realize that we have grandchildren. But inside, we are the age we always were. That is our secret.

> The wind is in from Africa
> Last night I couldn't sleep
> Oh, you know it sure is hard to leave here Carey
> But it's really not my home

It is July and I am driving to Cape Cod. My husband is beside me. Our teenage daughter is in the back seat, listening to the lyrics of her life on her iPod. And I am singing "Carey." The words are simple, direct. Young. They are a warm wind full of possibilities. I feel them. I turn them over and over, playing with them. They transport and transcend. I am as young now as I was when I first sang them. I will always be that young. That is my secret.

> Come on down to the Mermaid Café
> And I will
> Buy you a bottle of wine
> And we'll laugh
> And toast to nothing
> And smash our empty glasses down

Before I was a professor, before I pondered if "Mermaid Café" is an internal rhyme, before I owned a garrison colonial in a pleasant suburb, I owned a guitar. I was twenty-something, then thirty-something, and I sang and people listened.

My voice was sweet and playful, so unlike the serious young woman who owned it. My life was responsibility; "Carey" was possibility. When I sang it, I knew that one day I would stand on a beach in Crete and feel the warm, gritty wind that blows across the Mediterranean from the Libyan Desert. Perhaps I still shall. This is not nostalgia, a door to the past. "Carey" is a door to the present, to life, to possibility, to love, to who we are when we do not look in mirrors or at calendars. It is not perfection. There is the grit of a life in progress. "Carey" opens the door to who we are, not who we have become.

My husband listens. He knows my secret. In fact, it is his secret, too. The ages that we wear for the world are not real. This is real.

> Maybe I'll go to Amsterdam
> Maybe I'll go to Rome
> And rent me a grand piano
> And put some flowers 'round my room

One day we will live by the sea and walk in the warm sand and drink wine and laugh and be, once again, as young as we still are. We shall. And I will sing a sweet song of tomorrows and tomorrows into the warm evening breeze, because that is what young people do. That is what "Carey" does.

We cross the bridge that takes us from the mainland to the Cape. "Carey" is with us. "Carey" is always with us. Sis would understand.

BLUE

Blue
Songs are like tattoos
You know I've been to sea before
Crown and anchor me
Or let me sail away

Hey Blue here is a song for you
Ink on a pin
Underneath the skin
An empty space to fill in

Well there're so many sinking now
You've got to keep thinking
You can make it thru these waves
Acid, booze, and ass
Needles, guns, and grass
Lots of laughs
Lots of laughs

Everybody's saying that
Hell's the hippest way to go
Well I don't think so
But I'm gonna take a look around it though

Blue
Here is a shell for you
Inside you'll hear a sigh
A foggy lullaby
There is your song from me

INSPIRED BY THE SONG "BLUE"

RANDY JOHNSON

i am 17
and there is a song underneath the tongue
piano keys and nerve endings
the blue ache of the sky
the gray weight of the waves
pulling me under into a pain so pure
so bone close
even skin disappears

and then there is a beloved sea swell sweetness
love and loss and love again

40 years later,
such cruel arithmetic,
blue malaise
giving way to corrosive coral reefs
to bang your body on
"acid, booze and ass"
stories of windswept waves
transitory thumbprint at the scene of the crime
"needles, guns and grass"
no laughter from these damaged waters

at 17
i remember
how thin the song was to me then
now it is fatted out with experience
and silence
at the edges of things
love and loss and love again

there is a song underneath my tongue
i am an ocean talking to itself

"Blue" is a song, a deep unregarded river, that has pulsed in my veins for over forty years. It is a rich exploration of relationships set against the dark background of its times.

The commitment dance vs. freedom flight plays out in metaphors from the sea. The poet Octavio Paz once wrote: "The truth is I never understood anyone's messages, only the ocean existed," which I, in my ocean love, particularly embrace. Few songwriters have dived into the intricacies, ambivalences and complexities of relationships and love as Joni Mitchell has; the freedoms they give and the freedoms they take away. "Blue" is one of those songs and has served as a soundtrack for many of my own relationships. Not only has the full body of her work been a constant wellspring of inspiration, but I have steeped myself in her visual art as well. Never one to follow the conventions of the art world, she has adhered to her own sensibilities and has created visual equivalencies of the best of her writing.

CALIFORNIA

Sitting in a park in Paris, France
Reading the news and it sure looks bad
They won't give peace a chance
That was just a dream some of us had
Still a lot of lands to see
But I wouldn't want to stay here
It's too old and cold and settled in its ways here
Oh, but California
California I'm coming home
I'm going to see the folks I dig
I'll even kiss a Sunset pig
California I'm coming home

I met a redneck on a Grecian isle
Who did the goat dance very well
He gave me back my smile
But he kept my camera to sell
Oh the rogue, the red red rogue
He cooked good omelettes and stews
And I might have stayed on with him there
But my heart cried out for you, California
California, I'm coming home
Make me feel good rock 'n' roll band
I'm your biggest fan
California I'm coming home

Oh it gets so lonely
When you're walking
And the streets are full of strangers
All the news of home you read
Just gives you the blues
Just gives you the blues

So I bought me a ticket
I caught a plane to Spain
Went to a party down a red dirt road
There were lots of pretty people there
Reading Rolling Stone, reading Vogue
They said "How long can you hang around?"
I said a week—maybe two
Just until my skin turns brown
Then I'm going home to California
California I'm coming home
Will you take me as I am
Strung out on another man
California I'm coming home

Oh it gets so lonely
When you're walking
And the streets are full of strangers
All the news of home you read
More about the war
And the bloody changes
Oh will you take me as I am?
Will you take me as I am?
Will you?
Will you take me as I am?
Take me as I am

CALIFORNIA: AGAINST AUTOBIOGRAPHY

EDMOND CHIBEAU

To get lost in all the autobiographical elements and confessional details of even Joni Mitchell's most intimately personal work is a mistake. To tease out the names of people, or editions of *Rolling Stone*, that she refers to in the song "California" is an easy way to seem knowledgeable about her writing, but it avoids coming to terms with what really touches us about the song.

"California" is self-disclosure as artistic structure, not mere autobiography. The early listeners who made Joni Mitchell a big star were not interested in her private life but in her art. By "art" I mean her audio recordings: her music and lyrics. Only later did her lifestyle and long list of famous lovers become part of the oeuvre.

But what we can get right away, even if we don't know her personal history or the names of her lovers, is the piercing intimacy that is carried through her lyrics and the emotional inflections of her voice. Through her voice, she is able to smile ruefully at her own mistakes and share with us the acceptance of the fact that she gets it wrong, suffers for it, and somehow forgives herself and keeps on going. Her humor isn't jab-you-in-the-ribs, forced funny, but rather a bemused, ironic recognition of the mistakes we make, sometimes repeatedly, as we try to figure out the life we lead.

If this were not the case, then the songs from *Blue* would only be of interest to those who had been to the town of Matala on Crete in 1970, or the particular Spanish Island of Ibiza. The fact that the story is autobiographical obscures the fact that she builds a character that has the sensual particulars of her trip abroad in 1970.

She becomes a character in the song "California." The story may be from her life but she is "the storyteller," not the private Joni that she is when she's not performing.

The historical details may be about Joni on vacation in a particular place in a particular year, but the interior revelations are universal, and they are presented by the voice she has adopted for this performance.

If autobiography is the primary criterion of the value of poetry, then "Woodstock" is a failed work. She did not perform at Woodstock and she did not attend the concert. But her song captured the moment, and shared what she captured with the rest of the world.

Is "Urge For Going" about leaving cold, flat, middle-of-the-country, Canada, or about ending her marriage to Chuck Mitchell, or is it about an inner restlessness that drives human beings to discover what is over the next mountain, or across the next valley? Is "California" about a visit to Crete, or Paris, or Ibiza, or is it about coming home to Southern California? I am sure it's about all of those things and many more. To try to pin it down is a disservice to both the composer and the listener.

The lyric is about those things and a hundred other images, ideas, words, and desires that flitted across her consciousness and her subconscious at the moment of creation. The velocity of the poetry in "California" and on the whole *Blue* album is spellbinding. It moves from idea to idea, from rhetorical technique to rhetorical technique so quickly that we continue to listen and to ask ourselves, "What will she say next?"

In many ways "California" is a place poem, or should I say, a "places poem"; it is about several places, but most of all it is about places in her heart. She speaks of Paris, Ibiza and the town of Matala on the Island of Crete. But those places are used to bring into high relief the world of California.

For her, California is a lover, a friend, a place in the sun and a place of refuge where she can feel at home. Where she can be among like-minded souls that will take her as she is, hung up on another man.

In this song Joni is everywhere. She travels in place, time, emotion, and language. She can bi-locate at the drop of a metaphor or the flatting of a seventh. It does no good to try to fix these lyrics, or this writer, in one spot. She is changing, growing, moving. And we move along with her.

Her music and lyrics and voice trade off which will carry the main thrust, the main meaning, of the passage. Sometimes it is the meaning of the words, sometimes the intonation and implication of the voice, and sometimes it is the surprise of hearing that note, or that sound, at this point in the piece.

We can say that her blue period began with the album *Blue* in 1971, a time when she was intimately autobiographical and excruciatingly honest. Why would someone who is not Canadian, not a musician and not a woman identify with Mitchell's work? The answer is that the work must be good enough to transcend those accidental attributes, and touch a deep and universal nerve. If her work in the *Blue* period is merely therapeutic, confessional, autobiography, then she is just some local talent who got lucky. But if it opens us up to ourselves, through a kind of total artwork that includes voice, tuning, attitude, painting and all the devices of poetry, then she is a world class artist who can and will hold her own across space and time, even with those who are ignorant of her biography and only know the work itself. What is most specific and most particular can reveal an intimacy and insight into the shared moments of our humanity.

Books and articles have been written about the bearded lover on Crete who "kept my camera to sell," and about her being so happy to be home that she would embrace a police officer on Sunset Strip and "kiss a Sunset pig." But in uncovering every autobiographical particular we lose our feeling for the linguistic multiplicity and emotional nuance of her work.

Mitchell hit the trifecta of musical skill, poetic ability and an intimate voice that draws us in, but all of that is almost worthless without the insight into the human condition that makes her work universal.

Do we need to know the name of the person she was speaking to when she said, "Will you take me as I am / Strung out on another man"? Of course not! It was California, it was all of her rock star lovers, it was a state of mind, it was me accepting the one I loved who was coming back, and maybe it was you, coming home.

"YOUR LIFE BECOMES A TRAVELOGUE" WITH JONI MITCHELL

PATTI PARLETTE

Oh, but California!

When I was in seventh grade (November, 1966), my family (mother, father and three younger brothers) moved to California from Stamford, Connecticut. It was a dream-come-true for a twelve-year-old girl during the golden days of the Beach Boys. "I wish they all could be California girls"—and I was about to become one! I remember driving up Highway 101 to our new home in Santa Barbara, singing "Good Vibrations" along with the radio. The following summer was the Summer of Love. Although it was born and flourished in San Francisco, it definitely trickled down to Santa Barbara. "Lying on the beach with the transistor going" with all the great music of that summer was a magical experience. I had become a music lover when the Beatles first appeared on The Ed Sullivan Show on my tenth birthday, and "Sgt. Pepper's Lonely Hearts Club Band" was playing, along with Jefferson Airplane's "White Rabbit" and the Doors' "Light My Fire" and on and on. I had my first kiss on the beach (queue up Lesley Gore's "California Nights"). I was coming of age in paradise!

We lived there for a year, a month and three days. (You count the days you live in paradise.) Then came the unbearable news: my dad was being transferred back to Connecticut. In the middle of eighth grade—four days before Christmas—we moved back. While I had been homesick for my hometown and my old friends, this was "a rough road to travel."

I remember going to visit my old school, St. Mary's. My friends told me that Sister Mary Loyola said, after my visit, "Isn't it a shame what happened to that nice Patti Parlette?" Ha. I guess she didn't like my hot pink and orange mini dress with the daisies all over it, and my hoop earring and "eyelids painted green." I was a suddenly a stranger in my hometown.

We ended up moving a little north of Stamford. I wouldn't be with my old friends after all. My first day at Monroe Middle School was the day before my fourteenth birthday. I remember standing in front of my new class, being introduced by the vice principal as "Patti Parlette, our new student from California." It's not easy to change schools, let alone coasts, in those formative years, but my California Girl mystique helped me fit in pretty quickly. I made new friends but could not let go of my longing for California and the friends I had made there. Letters flew back and forth from coast to coast.

I remember sitting in my bedroom, listening to Judy Collins' *Wildflowers*. Two songs in particular jumped out at me: "Both Sides Now" and "Michael from Mountains." And then, one day, along came Joni! My new friend Olana gave me *Song To A Seagull*. The words spoke to me in new ways. It was not just music to my ears. It was poetry. A new lyrical language! "Oh, speak again, bright angel!"

Press the rewind button, please: I had to absorb every word, every phrase. I love languages and always have. When I was much younger, third or fourth grade, I fell in love with Hayley Mills and her lovely British accent. I would imitate it all the time. I showed an early interest in other languages, too, so in fourth grade my Aunt Pat gave me the gift of after-school French language classes. I loved it!

I played *Song to a Seagull* over and over on my little blue plastic record player. I soaked up all of those songs. "Out of the city / And down to the seaside / To sun on my shoulders and wind in my hair." Joni brought me back to California in ways no one else could. In May 1969 came *Clouds* and the "Both Sides Now" I had heard first from Judy. April 1970 brought *Ladies of the Canyon*, and I was drinking it all in. "Woodstock." "Willy." "The Priest."

One day in sophomore English class, Mrs. Carney handed out a list of essay topics. Scrolling through it, nothing grabbed me, until I saw this: "We are stardust / We are golden / And we've got to get ourselves / Back to the garden." Sweet inspiration! I was off and running, and wrote my Joni heart and mind out. I wish I still had that essay. I would love to see what "sophomore jive" I wrote. I do remember that I got an A. Also, that sophomore year, I was chairwoman of our class dance. In those days, we named our dances, and I remember insisting on "Night In The City." (I was also the chair of our freshman class dance, which we named "Purple Haze" because everyone loved Jimi Hendrix. Did we listen to the physics teacher who told us that the dry ice we bought would not rise up in our wished-for haze under the purple spotlights, but would just melt into puddles on the floor? Nope. "But you know, life is for learning.")

As a junior, I took creative writing with Mr. O'Conner. He was so cool. One day he said we all had to do oral presentations. Once again, we were presented with a list of suggested topics. Deja vu, "like lightning from above," I was struck. "The Impressionism of Joni Mitchell." What fun I had with that one! "You know life is for learning," so I started reading about Monet and Manet and Renoir and Corot, staring at their paintings and seeing the shadows and light and impressions. Joni's songs suddenly became not just poetry and music to me, but paintings! "Painting with words and music." I remember carrying the albums *Song To A Seagull*, *Clouds* and *Ladies of the Canyon*, along with bulky coffee table books about French Impressionism, under my arms onto the yellow school bus. Another A. I was becoming a Joni scholar!

As you all know, the next album was *Blue*. Deep breath. Wow! These songs grabbed me like no others. I was seventeen, just finishing my junior year, fresh off that "Impressionism of Joni Mitchell" presentation. My immediate favorite (again, "lightning from above!") was "California." And "Blue." "Crown and anchor me"—oh, the lyrics! The longing! I would live them out perfectly in just a few years, when I would study abroad in... Paris, France! "Songs are like tattoos."

For The Roses came out when I was a freshman at the University of Connecticut. I remember buying it at one of the two campus record stores, The Disc, and rushing back to my dorm room, Hurley 209, to play it. Joni was just getting better and better. I played it over and over, savoring every note and chord and word, but in my case, especially the words. As a language and lyrics person, I just loved her words, her poetry. They would "mainline to my blues" or joys or whatever I was feeling at any given moment. My next door neighbor was smitten with Loggins and Messina, and sometimes we would try to drown each other out. "Vahevalla, homeless sailor" versus "Lesson in survival, spinning out on turns that get you tough." That October, I started working for George McGovern's presidential campaign. He was my first political love. "Tin soldiers and Nixon coming?" No more Nixon! Joni and James Taylor and Carole King also supported him. Is that why I did? Surely, "The Judgment of the Moon And Stars" impelled me.

Court and Spark came out in January 1974. Back to the record store, racing home to my college apartment, tearing the cellophane off the album and getting sucked in again. "Down to You." "Free Man In Paris." "Help Me!" Since I was majoring in

German and French, I loved any reference Joni made to traveling or to other countries and cultures. I had already decided to spend my junior year in France, so "Free Man In Paris" really enhanced my anticipation. I saw Joni for the first time that February, at Woolsey Hall at Yale University. She was stardust. She was golden!

At the end of my sophomore year, one of my French professors suggested a trip to Quebec that summer (1974), as a prelude to France. As "une jeune fille bien rangée" (Simone de Beauvoir), I took the suggestion seriously. In late July, my boyfriend, two friends and I packed up camping equipment in our two vehicles. This was my first car, a used navy blue Volvo 144S that we had just bought from a Sociology professor at Yale. (The Yale/Joni connection sealed the deal for me.) I was really proud of it, and the "Impeach the President. Now More Than Ever" bumper sticker I had purchased for one dollar ("buy your dreams a dollar down") from a classified ad in *Rolling Stone*. When I saw the first road sign in French, I was so excited. "Pull over! I have to take a picture!" The sign merely said "Poulet Frite à la Kentucky," but I was thrilled to see French in action for the first time. We "camped out on the land" at Mont Tremblant, and then ventured into Montreal as our final jaunt before going back home. However, as John Lennon said: "Life is what happens to you when you're busy making other plans." I saw a poster in a window announcing that Joni Mitchell would be playing on August 4 at La Place des Nations. Stop. Buy two tickets! Our two friends had to go home, but I was not to be denied seeing Joni again. We were plumb out of cash. We found a phone booth and called our parents and begged for money. No "credit card eyes" for us. We had no credit cards then. We spent half a day driving up and down the railroad tracks looking for the Western Union Office, then more time finding a bank to cash the fifty dollar check. We had a cheap dinner in some Barangrill, gassed up the Volvo and bought a little bottle of Canadian whiskey for the concert (Now I'd say "Yuck!" but when in Canada...).

The concert was two days away. We had no money left, no place to stay and no food except for ketchup and peanut butter in the trunk. We parked the Volvo in some farmer's field and slept. The next morning, the day of the concert, we found ourselves stuck in the mud. Pushing the car out of the mud was impossible, but somehow we did it. We got on the island, saw the big metal "marbled bowling ball" from Expo 67, and finally found La Place des Nations on the other end of the island. We made it! But it was raining. Hard. And this was an outdoor concert. We waited on wet blankets with hundreds of others for hours. Concert time passed. Finally, the sun broke out, the gates opened and there was Joni! Fueled by that little bit of Canadian whiskey, I naturally was singing along until a gentle soul in front of me turned and asked: "Would you mind not singing? I came to hear Joni." Embarrassed and apologetic, I clapped my hand over my mouth and enjoyed the magical experience of seeing my idol in the flesh. She was beautiful in her white jeans and apricot blouse, with the wind whipping her long blonde hair, telling us about living in Canada, and the arbutus rustling and then singing about it. It was some enchanted evening and worth every sacrifice. Oh, Canada!

And then, it was finally time to live out "California." October 1974. "Sitting in a park in Paris, France, reading the news...." I was finally here! And Joni was with me every step of the way. I was soaking up all the art and culture and I had only read about, and was lucky to catch the *Centenaire de l'impressionnisme* exhibit on the Champs Elysees! At the same time, I was a little homesick. Sitting in Reid Hall, with Mme. Triantafalou trying to teach us French phonetics, I was scribbling out Joni lyrics on the graph paper in my blue cahier. We had little vacations, "so I bought me a ticket" (Eurail train pass), and "maybe I"ll go to Amsterdam, maybe I'll go to Rome." My roommate Christine had brought a little tape recorder with her so she could send tapes home to family and friends. We had one music cassette tape with us. Last Tango In Paris. Moody stuff. Not much comfort in that melancholy. So it was a special delight when my boyfriend sent me the newly released *Miles of Aisles* for Christmas. Then it was all Joni, all the time, all throughout Europe. She was my comfort and my strength and sweet inspiration that whole year. I loved France, and all of Europe, but Joni was right. It's pretty "old and cold and settled in its ways here." I longed for home, especially for California. "Oh, California."

Senior year, back at The University of Connecticut. *The Hissing of Summer Lawns*, November 1975. "Again and again the same situation." Back to the record store and racing home to the college apartment that I shared with four Deadheads. Ripped *Workingman's Dead* from the turntable, and was sucked in again. My housemates loved Joni, too (they had to, living with me), and I loved the Dead, too, but that winter it was the battle of the turntables. The first song, of course, mainlined to my recent experience in France. "In France they kiss on Main Street, amour, mama, not cheap display!" How I loved that one. But what is this "Jungle Line" song? Whoa, Joni. Where are we going now? Right around that time, my housemate Bob asked me if I wanted to go with him to meet some of his high school friends in another college apartment. One of their girlfriends, Janis, put *Blue* on the turntable, and turned to me to ask, "Do you like Joni Mitchell?" We've been best friends ever since. ("The gift goes on...." Twenty-five years later, Janis, her daughter Tara and I would gasp in delight together at the Oakdale Theater when Joni walked out on the stage: "There she is!")

Hejira comes out in November 1976. More Joni awesomeness. Even though I have "we don't need no piece of paper from the city hall, keeping us tied and true" ringing in my ears, my boyfriend and I decide to get married. So began my own personal *The Hissing of Summer Lawns.* We had two wonderful sons: Christopher in 1978 and Michael (from Mountains!) in 1984. While I still had Joni playing in my head, I'm sorry to say that I kind of lost her during those days of childrearing, "going round and round and round in the circle game" times two.

"The years spin by and now" the boys are twenty and thirty. College graduates, they're "grown and gone, like the turn of a page." Both are happily married, and I'm proud to share that at both of their weddings the mother of the groom dances were Joni songs. Now who does that? Neither were dance numbers, but I was not to be denied. Christopher and I went round and round and round to the "Circle Game," and Michael and I danced to "Michael From Mountains." The photographer, who turned out to be a Joni fan himself, was beaming on the sidelines.

Suddenly I have "time on my hands, no child to raise," so one day I type "Joni Mitchell" into my computer, when what should appear to my wondering eyes but jonimitchell.com and the Joni Mitchell Discussion List (JMDL). Now I'm back in Joni business! I have met so many wonderful souls on the JMDL. "Love is touching souls!" Some of my closest friends these days are JMDLers. Suffice it to say that being part of this wonderful community is just like going to California. I get to see the folks I dig. All the Joni people! "Will you take me as I am? Will you?" was the subject line of my first post to the JMDL near my fiftieth birthday, in 2004, and I have found my paradise. We talk all the time—on the phone, online and, finally, in person at the Joni Tribute at Carnegie Hall on February 1, 2006. I had to leave that celebration a little early, as my Dad was ailing in Utah. We lost him on February 11, and I remember some of his last words to me were: "Go to that Joni thing and have fun." The love and the comfort from what I have come to call my "Joniamigos" were such a blessing at that terrible time.

One of our Joniamigos once asked: "Does anyone ever get into trouble quoting Joni in love relationships?" It was then that I finally let what I now call my full-blown JMOCD (Joni Mitchell Obsessive Compulsive Disorder) out of the closet and wrote out a Joni riff like I never had before. All the Joni spirit that's inside of me finally became my new language! I quote her incessantly in everyday life. She has words that no other language has to express all human emotions. There's a Joni scene in the movie *Love Actually*, where Emma Thompson's character is listening to "River." Her two-timing husband asks, "What is this music?" Emma: "It's Joni Mitchell. She taught me how to feel. I love her. And true love lasts a lifetime." Well, Joni did not teach me how to feel beginning in eighth grade, but through her poetry and music she did teach me how to express those feelings, and for that I am forever grateful.

But to get back to the song "California," here is where it comes full circle. "One Week Last Summer," in 2011, there was a tribute to Joni at the Hollywood Bowl. "Joni's Jazz." Thanks to one of our Joniamigos, sixty-four JMDLers all met in the "City of the Fallen Angels." It was a huge Jonifest, as these meetings of hearts and minds are called. We all stayed at the same hotel and had a picnic in the park before the concert. After the tribute, in the following days, we had field trips to Laurel Canyon (we found Our House!), the ocean, Sunset Boulevard, and parties at the top of Topanga Canyon and in the Hollywood Hills. "No more Hollywood heartache, we got a break."

> Oh, but California
> California I'm coming home
> I'm going to see the folks I dig
> I'll even kiss a Sunset pig
> California I'm coming home

It was the time of my life. It recently occurred to me that the dates of those four days of peace and love and Joni music in L.A. are the same dates of Woodstock, many dim years ago: August 15-18, 1969. *Quelle* "we are stardust, we are golden" *coincidence*! We got ourselves back to the garden.

Who knows? I may not have been "sitting in a park in Paris, France" or have made it home to California to see "the folks I dig" if it weren't for Joni's constant lyrical and musical presence in my life. I certainly would not be the same person I am today without her entire rich and complex and brilliant oeuvre playing the soundtrack of my life. The impressionism of Joni Mitchell, indeed. With thanks to my first musical loves, the Beatles: "When I find myself in times of trouble, Joni Mitchell comforts me. Speaking words of wisdom, let it be." Thank you, Joni! "You are in my blood, you're like holy wine." I have drunk many cases of you, and I am—thanks to you—still on my feet. "A round resounding for you way up here" in New England!

RIVER

It's coming on Christmas
They're cutting down trees
They're putting up reindeer
And singing songs of joy and peace
Oh I wish I had a river
I could skate away on
But it don't snow here
It stays pretty green
I'm going to make a lot of money
Then I'm going to quit this crazy scene
Oh I wish I had a river
I could skate away on
I wish I had a river so long
I would teach my feet to fly
I wish I had a river
I could skate away on
I made my baby cry

He tried hard to help me
You know, he put me at ease
And he loved me so naughty
Made me weak in the knees
Oh, I wish I had a river
I could skate away on
I'm so hard to handle
I'm selfish and I'm sad
Now I've gone and lost the best baby
That I ever had
I wish I had a river
I could skate away on
Oh, I wish I had a river so long
I would teach my feet to fly

I wish I had a river
I could skate away on
I made my baby say goodbye

It's coming on Christmas
They're cutting down trees
They're putting up reindeer
And singing songs of joy and peace
I wish I had a river
I could skate
Away
On

JOURNALING "THE RIVER" (A FICTIONAL WORK)

WILLA CORRENTI

It is December 5, 1969, and I am at a Joni Mitchell concert at Symphony Hall in Boston with my boyfriend. He is Candace Bushnell's cousin, but I don't know that yet. No one knows that, for it is years before *Sex and the City* was even written, and we are only teenagers. My boyfriend is obsessed with Joni Mitchell, and when she walks on stage with her pale blonde hair falling to her waist and brushes it back with one delicate hand as she sits down at the piano I feel somehow a slight tinge of jealousy. When the audience finally quiets and Joni starts to sing, I think first she is singing Judy Collins' songs but I have never heard them sung like this before. In fact, I have never really felt "Chelsea Morning" or "Both Sides Now" and I enter into a world of musical emotion lifting me up and down with the soprano scales of Joni's clear staccato voice. I learn later that these weren't Judy Collin's songs at all but Joni's. The song "River" won't be written until 1971, but I am starting to flow with the intense ripples of Joni's music. And when the audience rises to its feet with thunderous applause for Joni, I am enthralled.

On hearing Joni Mitchell's song "River" for the first time, I flashback to being only five or six years old and my father telling me about living on the St Lawrence (in Quebec City, Canada) when he was a little boy, and how in winter the frozen river became a thoroughfare and means of transportation for them.

"I wish I had a river / I could skate away on"

Listening to the song on my small transistor radio, I think of how Joni is Canadian, too... and how the river therefore cannot just be a means of escape but also a going towards something.

"I wish I had a river so long / I would teach my feet to fly"

I want so desperately to be grown up and leave my home and town. But I also want to move to Boston and to become a famous poet or writer of song lyrics. I want to go, I want to come, just like the river in Joni's song ebbs and flows and curves around bends leaving us curious to see what is next, just out of sight.

The summer of '71, the same season Joni's "River" song debuts on the *Blue* album, I find myself pregnant. Teenage and unmarried, I am way too young to be a mother. I struggle with my decision. I feel so alone, afraid to tell my mom, even my best friend. Years later, watching a documentary about Joni and her lost daughter re-uniting, I think on how it describes Joni Mitchell's similar painful situation and parallel struggle: Joni, at an early age, alone and pregnant, perhaps at night spilling the conflicted torment of her heart out, both in scribbled lines and in guitar chords. Both of us partially wanting to have our baby but also not wanting to have this biological role determine the fate and outcome of our lives. Now, years later, I begin to realize how we were as much builders of the new era for women as we were victims of it. Finally, an older friend helps me arrange an abortion and drives me west to New York. Coming back after, Joni's "River" song plays on the car radio and I hear with new poignancy the lines: "Now I've gone and lost the best baby / That I ever had." It could be a man/boy, most probably is. But there, aching in the back seat of the car where I am laying, my stomach cramping and my lower back hurting, I think Joni is singing about a baby. My baby? Her baby? All lost babies.

A few days later, I jot down some lines of poetry. Maybe someday I can play guitar like Joni and put them to music.

> Crying to New York
> coming up the stairs
> into a dark corridor
> and having life in you
> and wanting to die
> a little
> someone's hand reaches out
> and she says
> its not so bad...

I call her "Dana." I don't want to make her real, but I can't help it. I struggle with my thoughts... finally write a poem for her... and put her away.

> *FOR DANA*

> Poor little child
> when I put you away
> from me
> I couldn't allow myself
> to even feel
> the loss
> of you...
> to say
> that you ever were...
> I didn't know
> then
> I had also put
> aside
> a gentle part of me
> the light in my teenage eyes
> doesn't shine
> in the glossy photos
> taken after...
> turning the album page
> two years later
> in my arms I cradle
> my new baby daughter
> and my lips smile

for the camera
my fingers gently caress her
but
on looking closer
my dark eyes
seem somehow somber...
I was only just then
beginning
to know
the most infinitesimal
sense
of my loss
of you.

Like Joni, I am way too young, living with a man who doesn't get my sensitive, artistic nature—and like her I will have to leave him to mature and find myself.

A few years later I give birth to a blue-eyed, blonde baby girl, born with the sun in Cancer. I am Joni perhaps, if she had kept her baby or had another one right after to make up for the hole in her heart. Other young women friends of mine back then had done this. Years later one even told me: "I later had three babies to make up for the three I had lost." I sublimate my art to my little girl, but at the same time in some weird symbiotic way it is she who begins, through her pure awe at the world, to put me back in touch with myself. So we finger-paint together and dance in the early spring mud and begin to sing simple stories to each other... But I am a full time mom and going to school, and sometimes late at night, almost falling asleep over a psychology textbook, I listen to Joni singing and really "wish I had a river I could skate away on."

I sing or hum along with Joni's song, and, in my life, it becomes for me like the golden thread of Indian Literature holding stories together.

"I'm so hard to handle / I'm selfish and I'm sad"

My daughter has just turned two when my old boyfriend Mick, Candace's cousin, gets in touch with me. He wants to start over again. Being separated, I decide to spend some time with him. When it doesn't somehow feel right, I must tell him, find the right words. To get the mood, I listen to "River"; play it over concentrating on the line: "I broke my baby's heart."

I struggle with the realization that even though it hurts like hell to be the one left, it is even harder to be the one doing the leaving. You are the one who now must make the ultimate decision and take full responsibility for any consequences and regrets, as well as having the knowledge that you have caused real emotional pain to someone you cared deeply about. Still, it is taking control of one's life. It is being the actor rather than the reactor, much as other young women of this same time period are struggling to find their real selves hidden beneath all the restrictions society has formerly imposed on females.

I imagine myself skating away on a river in smooth purposeful strokes. And so I find my courage and tell him "goodbye," actually happily surprised afterwards at the strength I have found in myself.

"But it don't snow here / It stays pretty green."

This line so perfectly describes, for me, the decade of the 1980s.

In my mind I equate the snow with a kind of ethereal art—a frozen rebirth in its icy beauty. But it also carries with it in its austere frigid flakes a kind of erotic sadness.

I feel it is like my writing, essentially dormant and emerging, a line here and there, only when allowed to break briefly through the surface of my everyday life.

A life, rich in its own tired fulfillment, I equate to the "green" of Joni's line. Joni, in Californian sunshine, missing the frozen, white beauty of her Canadian homeland. Me, having remarried with two more babies, totally submerged in family and work life, missing even the time to listen to my muse.

Finally, in the mid 1990s, as my children get a little older with growing independence, I return to school and, ultimately, myself. Joni, ironically, returns to a part of herself when she is reunited with her long lost daughter after many years on the road singing songs, which in turn have helped her audience to reach into their own souls.

I begin to write in Wally Lamb's creative writing seminar. On the first weekend of the semester, I break from a homework writing exercise to look for quarters for the washer and dryer, and then reference that incident in my work. Wally loves it! In our first class journal entry, nervous after years out of school, I quickly jot down to excuse myself: "For some time now my writing has been confined to grocery lists & notes to my daughters."

Sometimes, as I reach for ideas to write about, I begin to dig deep and start to sense my own hibernating creativity and begin to urge it gently awake. For inspiration I listen to Joni's *Blue* album—its melodies giving me back the feel of my early self. Sensing its embers beginning to smolder, I start to realize that creative passion is indeed timeless and ageless.

In the 2000s I am still working on my poetry, and my first novel is finally complete. There have been endless sessions with Wally Lamb helping edit it, and countless readings of it at my bi-monthly writers group, culminating in numerous rewrites. My fingers cramped and my eyes circled from late nights typing and re-typing at my keyboard. Now it is time to take my manuscript on the road so to speak—to find an agent, that elusive dream personage, who hopefully will secure one of the big name publishers for my work.

As rejection slips start to come in, even after some initial responses asking to see more, I realize something Joni already knew in her "River" song—the muse inspires the artistic work, but it is a hard commercial being that does the selling of it. These two realities are often at odds.

"I'm going to make a lot of money / Then I'm going to quit this crazy scene"

Here Joni so well portrays the timeless struggle for all artists of staying true to oneself and one's work, or selling out for money. At the Kentucky Women's Writers' Conference in spring of 2005, I had a conversation with guest writer Candace Bushnell about how she was able to get a perfect intersection (for her) of creativity and marketability. As a struggling writer trying to get my first novel published, this so fascinated me!

Joni's lyrics are still so relevant, even today in 2011, as recently in a Howard Stern interview, I heard Lady Gaga saying how some artists/singers have one great hit and then, spoiled by the lure of money, write to the market, think they deserve everything and become mediocre.

As I continue writing poetry and fiction and struggle to get an agent, I question my marketability when I am told that my ethnic novel "although well written doesn't fit any particular niche." And I question, albeit briefly, if I need to sound like pop writers and ignore my own voice in order to find a publisher. Somehow Joni never settled but always heard her muse! She becomes like my talisman.

It is December 2008. I have just picked up my college age daughter at the train station. It is the start of her Christmas break. She chats excitedly as she turns the radio dial. She comments how there is nothing good on radio and plugs in her iPod.

The faint refrain of "Jingle Bells" begins playing...

My daughter exclaims "Mom, I love this song! Just listen to the words!"

The high soprano voice rises over the music...

"It's coming on Christmas / They're cutting down trees"

I am suddenly struck with the realization that Joni doesn't just belong to her own generation but to the next, and the "river" flows on...

RIVER

JILL ROBINSON

I was ten years old and growing up in the U.K. when Joni Mitchell released "Both Sides Now." I remember her beautiful, haunting lyrics through a childhood that saw Dad struggling to raise my sister Anne and I from when I was about nine years old.

We were babies when mum had died, and Dad had taken us on as best he could until the challenges of looking after two such young daughters, coupled with indescribable grief for the "best woman in the world," saw him looking to his brother for help. So, for the next few years, until we were a reasonable age for Dad to take us back, we lived with our devoted Auntie Floss and Uncle Les. Caring as he was, a forty-five-year gap between his daughters and himself saw an "old school" upbringing for Anne and me, and so it was that I turned to animals and music—and found a passion for both that would see a love affair until this day.

Hearing Joni's music today carries me nostalgically back to those early years—and makes me a little homesick for the U.K. considering that I now divide my time between Hong Kong, China and Vietnam heading up the Animals Asia Foundation.

Here, our projects focus on bringing dog and cat consumption to an end, improving the welfare of animals in captivity, and ending the truly horrific practice of bear farming in China and Vietnam. The bear farming industry sees thousands of bears literally "milked" for their bile endlessly and cruelly throughout their lives, through painful and invasive means, until they die agonizing deaths from diseases such as liver cancer and peritonitis.

In Hong Kong, one of Joni's most famous tracks, "Big Yellow Taxi," has become an emblem song during protests against the building of luxury flats and a marina on a twenty-six hectare site on Lamma Island. The Eco Education and Resources Centre and Green Power, who found that even the slightest development bringing only light pollution (whatever that means) would harm marine life in southern Lamma, surveyed the site. There, three endangered species struggle to survive: the Romer's tree frog, green turtle and finless porpoise, which would all be threatened should the developers move in. "Big Yellow Taxi" from 1970, with its famous line "they paved paradise and put up a parking lot," couldn't be more apt some forty years later on a continent far away from where Joni crafted this fine environmental song.

Today, while I still love "Both Sides Now" and "Big Yellow Taxi," it is "River," released on the *Blue* album in 1971, that has become my favourite track of them all.

"River" is a song that makes me smile and cry all in one, encapsulating so many emotions that I hardly know where to begin. Perhaps it's the novelty of a Christmas song—one of my favourite times of the year, where my sister and I endlessly spoil her daughter Nicole throughout the festive days. Or perhaps it encapsulates the passion of that one special relationship: the dizzy headless days of love and, finally, the cold reality of mourning something from the past that, wonderful as it was, has died.

Thank you, Joni, for your life well lived, and in gratitude for the arcs of emotion whenever your voice reaches out across the globe.

A CASE OF YOU

Just before our love got lost you said
"I am as constant as a northern star"
And I said "Constantly in the darkness
Where's that at?
If you want me I'll be in the bar"
On the back of a cartoon coaster
In the blue TV screen light
I drew a map of Canada
Oh Canada
With your face sketched on it twice

You are in my blood like holy wine
You taste so bitter and so sweet
I could drink a case of you
Darling
And I'd still be on my feet
I would still be on my feet

I am a lonely painter
I live in a box of paints
I'm frightened by the devil
And I'm drawn to those ones that ain't afraid
I remember that time you told me, you said
"Love is touching souls"
Surely you touched mine
'Cause part of you
Pours out of me
In these lines from time to time

You are in my blood like holy wine
You taste so bitter and so sweet
I could drink a case of you
Darling
And I would still be on my feet
I would still be on my feet

I met a woman
She had a mouth like yours
She knew your life
She knew your demons and your deeds
And she said
"Go to him
Stay with him if you can
But be prepared to bleed"

But you are in my blood
You're my holy wine
You're so bitter
Bitter and so sweet
I could drink a case of you
Darling
And I'd still be on my feet
I would still be on my feet

CAFETERIA (A CASE OF YOU)

MICHAEL CORRENTI

"Things are a little crazy right now. You have my card, why don't you give us a try again in the spring?"

"I will." I shook the manager's hand and took my sample bag off the table. "Thanks again for your time." We stepped into the cluttered upstairs hallway and he gestured toward the back stairwell.

"No need to go through the sales floor again—this one'll spit ya out right on the street."

"Got it."

The faint voices from the store grew louder as I made my way down, then were cut off with a thud as the heavy service door closed itself behind me.

It was a couple weeks into February, and 40th Street was like a wind tunnel, cold rain whipping along the block toward Park Avenue. A year earlier I would have been viewing this storm from a classroom; now I was in it, crisscrossing the city each day, having meetings in back rooms and upstairs offices, securing every possible inch of shelf space.

One last appointment waited at a building several blocks away. I had just enough time to get there and stop for a late lunch in the lobby before the meeting started. In this weather an umbrella could do little more than protect the very top of one's head, so I moved fast, covering the distance in just a few minutes and ducking inside the lobby.

The food court was unkempt by late afternoon, hours removed from the lunch crowd and, like a typical office building eatery, not expecting much activity until morning. Cellophane wrappers dotted the floor and several unoccupied tables. Part lobby and part cafeteria, the atrium was the first thing to greet visitors—straight ahead from the entrance was a dull grey bank of elevators to the office suites above, while a line of shops hugged the wall and wrapped around the entire space. A large opening in the center revealed the dining area on the lower level.

I ordered my food and waited behind a middle-aged businesswoman who was leaving the checkout with a bottled drink and a sandwich. She crossed the room, stopped at the bar-style seating against a bare wall and settled in. A young man in a suit sat several chairs away, briefcase next to him on the table, devouring his meal as if he did not know when the next opportunity would come.

My purchase complete, I took my place at a table near the others. There was no audible conversation, save the murmurs of a janitor talking to an unseen acquaintance through an open doorway in one corner.

A grand piano sat at the base of a large column in the center of the dining area with a sign hanging above that read:
PLEASE DO NOT TOUCH—PIANO RESERVED FOR SCHEDULED PERFORMERS

A thump interrupted the quiet, from the direction of the escalator. A dark haired woman was descending with a large shopping bag. Expensive clothes did little to disguise her ragged visage. Several seconds before arriving at the lower floor she started shifting her weight, then leapt to the ground as her step slid down into the machinery. She made her way across the room, letting her hand lightly glide across the piano keys as she passed. She did not buy anything; rather she walked directly toward the bar and sat two places to the right of the businesswoman.

"Do you spend a lot of time in this neighborhood?"

The businesswoman nearly jumped at the question.

"Excuse me?"

"I'm sorry, I should have said hello first. Are you familiar with this area?"

"Yes, I actually work upstairs. What are you looking for?"

"Well, I-I'm not exactly sure. I am working through this thing. It is really... the past few weeks have been very difficult for me. I'm Debbie."

The businesswoman, her expression somewhere between sympathetic and cautious, turned to face Debbie.

"Well I don't know if it's what you need, but there is this very lovely church just several blocks away, I go there from time to time, even if I have a bit of extra time during my break, to sit and think about things."

"A church? Near here?"

"Yes, it's very beautiful. I think you might find some peace there."

"I spent so much time in my youth at this old, run-down but exquisite church just downtown!" Debbie laughed at herself. "Wow, so much time there. And it did bring me comfort. Not from silent reflection, no, they used to let us perform there. I would sing."

The businesswoman had fully turned back toward her meal by now and was glancing at an abandoned newspaper to her left.

"I sang first for myself, then in two different bands. One ended 'cause we just couldn't make it pay. You can live in a basement, but it still has a price. The other, the lead guy let me go when we broke up. You should have heard us; we had some really interesting things going on. Bending influences into something really special."

The businesswoman looked up from the paper for a moment. "That church, the one I mentioned, it's just a couple blocks away, straight up Third."

Debbie paused for a moment, looked down into her shopping bag and then back up at the businesswoman.

"Now me and Joni Mitchell!"

The man in the suit looked up, "You knew Joni Mitchell?"

"I was her!"

"What?" The businesswoman turned again to look at Debbie.

"How do you mean?" asked the man. Debbie looked him in the eyes this time.

"Have you seen my old red Gibson?"

"Uh, no. My dad had something along those lines."

Debbie broke eye contact with him as she shifted in her chair.

"Late one night in a beer bar I met this man. He was confused, thinking seriously to drop out of law school... to follow his dreams. Music and poetry. He showed me his notebook, he drew me in. He asked me out. But he seemed so dark and unsettled. I rejected him. I was looking for a more dynamic type, the ones on their way! You know them! He had sensitive eyes. Like magnets they pulled you in. Still I said to myself, I don't need that." She stopped. She took a breath and sang softly in a much clearer voice.

"You are in my blood like holy wine / You taste so bitter and so sweet"

Again, she stopped herself.

"Regrets. But I wasn't her! And I couldn't ever be not her! What's that song? She said it! Something like..."

She began to hum, then shook her head and began singing a different melody. She stopped once more, as a smile passed quickly across her face, like a break of sunlight through a cluster of pines. She began to recite the words, softly at first, then rose from her seat and collected her belongings as she repeated the line, growing louder as she walked away.

"I could drink a case of you / Darling / And I would still be on my feet"

My story was inspired by Joni Mitchell's "A Case of You." I view the song as a bittersweet remembrance of a lost relationship. While the relationship has ended, the passion is still very real: "Part of you / Pours out of me / In these lines from time to time."

The winter after I graduated from college, I was working as a marketer for a new product in New York. One cold February afternoon between sales meetings in midtown, with wind and rain blowing through the streets, I ducked inside the Citigroup Center for a cup of coffee.

As I sat down at a corner table, I noticed a businesswoman taking a late lunch nearby. A second woman, dressed in expensive but mismatched clothing, entered and began asking questions of the businesswoman. In a desperate tone, she inquired about which church she might be able to visit nearby and then continued the conversation until long after the businesswoman had clearly lost interest. With potted trees framing the two of them, and due to the erratic way the lonely woman moved, the scene took on a strange theatrical quality.

I found myself thinking of this moment. Perhaps, some forty years prior, this woman may have come to New York as a musician, with dreams of finding success. Further, she may have experienced lost love much like that of the narrator in "A Case of You," and perhaps this could be the alternate future of that narrator. My short story is the result.

BE PREPARED TO BLEED

BRENT CALDERWOOD

> "A poem is human inside talking to human inside. It may also be reasonable person
> talking to reasonable person, but if it is not inside talking to inside, it is not a poem."
>
> —Donald Hall, *Claims for Poetry*

I was seventeen when I first heard "A Case of You."

It was 1994. Bill Clinton had just been elected, *Turbulent Indigo*—Joni Mitchell's fifteenth album—had just been released and "gay youth" was a new term on the political landscape. The liberation movements of the '70s combined with AIDS education in the '80s meant that kids were coming out at younger and younger ages, and when I met my friend Danny at a youth group in Berkeley, I learned that I wasn't the only person like me. But being a "gay youth" wasn't the only thing we had in common—we were both listening to *Turbulent Indigo* on our Sony Walkmans. As kids who had grown up in the shadow of AIDS and had only heard stories about the Sexual Revolution, the track "Sex Kills" spoke to our sense of confusion about the times in which we were coming out and coming of age.

Soon, I was meeting Danny every Sunday at his house in Oakland, where we sat on the floor in front of a cable-spool coffee table, lit incense and devoured his mother's giant vinyl collection. We pored over covers of Joni's early songs by Ian and Sylvia, Fairport Convention and Buffy Sainte-Marie. During one of these visits, Danny played Tom Rush's version of "Urge for Going"; Danny's mom remembered having heard Joni's own version of the song on a midnight radio program when she was in college, but we couldn't find any other proof that Joni had recorded the song. (As it turned out, Joni had recorded "Urge for Going" for *Blue*, some four years after writing it, but it was traded out to make room for "The Last Time I Saw Richard"; it was later released as a B-side on the 45 for "You Turn Me On, I'm a Radio" and later still on her *Hits* album.)

As a surprise for Danny's birthday, I took out a classified ad (a relic that's gone the way of cable-spool coffee tables and Walkmans) in Berkeley's free weekly paper, The East Bay Express. A week later, the ad was answered by Wally Breese, an avid Joni collector—a completist, really. The following year, Wally would become the founding webmaster of JoniMitchell. com before succumbing to cancer.

On Danny's eighteenth birthday, we made the trek across the Bay Bridge to San Francisco, where we met Wally at his apartment, lined from floor to ceiling with Joni bootlegs, books and concert posters. He thrilled us with rarities, including that recording of "Urge for Going," a demo of Joni's very first composition from 1965, "Day After Day," and a live performance of "A Case of You" from 1971, just a few months before *Blue* was released—and five years before either of his visitors had been born.

After fiddling with the droning strings of her dulcimer, I heard Joni sing these lines:

> Just before our love got lost you said
> "I am as constant as a northern star"
> And I said "Constantly in the darkness
> Where's that at?
> If you want me I'll be in the bar"
> On the back of a cartoon coaster
> In the blue TV screen light
> I drew a map of Canada
> Oh Canada
> With your face sketched on it twice

At seventeen, I'd only been into a bar once or twice, with the help of a driver's license I'd stolen from my brother. I didn't even know what a cartoon coaster was, much less the complex texture of an ended affair. But I knew that I was hearing something special, something deeply personal, something more than "You done me wrong, baby." Something bitter and sweet.

Eighteen years of bars and heartache later, "A Case of You" still elicits that original visceral, intuitive response. Eighteen years of writing and teaching later, I can also see the craft in "A Case of You," the work that went into its composition long after the muse left the room.

On its surface, "A Case of You" is accessible and infectious, even for a naïve teenager: a great opening riff, a story of lost love that (almost) anyone can relate to and a mesmerizingly hooky chorus that would be equally at home in songs by Willie Nelson, Cole Porter or the Beatles. Its scaffolding—verse-chorus-verse-chorus—is as normal and unobtrusive as the frame on a Van Gogh.

But that's where the simplicity ends. Although she'd already been playing with traditional verse structure in songs like "The Arrangement" on *Ladies of the Canyon*, "A Case of You" is one her first examples of what songwriters call "through-writing" and what poets call "enjambment"—that is, sentences that move through and past the end of the line rather than stopping there. A term that comes from the French word for leg, enjambment is a stepping over the line in one continuous movement. The effect is a plainspoken, "natural" sound—verses that are truly free, liberated from strict metrical expectations.

With "A Case of You," Joni's rhyme scheme, too, diverges from the norm. She eschews the syntactical inversions and mathematically precise rhymes of her earliest songs ("Cats come crying to the key and dry you will be in a towel or two" from "Michael from Mountains") in favor of this new style; in effect, she has moved from making delicate filigree to working with steel. Her songs, like their speaker, have gone through the fire, been hammered into shape, tempered and polished.

Towards the end of his life, Wally played Danny and me an even earlier recording of "A Case of You" than the one we'd heard on that first visit. Just back from her summer in Greece and Spain, Joni appeared on the 1970 television program *Folkways*. Tentatively starting off the familiar, climbing dulcimer riff and repeating it a few times, as if trying to recall her new lyrics, she sings:

Just before our ship got lost you said
"I am as constant as the northern star"
"You're silly as a northern fish" says I
"If you want me, I'll be in the bar"

Here it is: a gauntlet thrown down before fans and naysayers alike who assume that Joni Mitchell's songwriting is pure instinct or stream-of-consciousness, an unmitigated expurgation of personal experience. While it's true that many of her songs seem to be borne of fearless living and risk-taking, they are only brought to maturity through sweat and merciless, unsentimental revision. Her revisions to her songs are anything but arbitrary or merely intuitive: they are the choices of an artist in complete control of her craft.

By the time "A Case of You" appears on *Blue*, she has jettisoned the nautical theme, which overloads and competes with the overriding themes of art, blood, drinking, religion and Holy Communion. She's also done away with tidy end-rhymes and that archaic-sounding syntactical inversion, "says I." In fact, the only line she's kept intact is "'If you want me I'll be in the bar,'" which sets the tone for the rest of the song with a kind of unaffected, self-effacing truth-telling that's rarely heard in pop music. The song has been wiped clean of its "poetic" conceits so that it just is; its meter and rhyme scheme are given the ambivalent blur that suit a song about alcohol and heartache.

Whereas the early "nautical" version of "A Case of You" has a traditional balladic rhyme scheme of ABCB ("said/star/I/bar") in straightforward iambic tetrameter (a logical choice for a song that's mostly in 4/4 time), the rhymes in the finished version are intentionally ambiguous—everyone will have a slightly different perspective on what those rhymes are, like museum-goers seeing a painting from different vantage points.

Listen closely to "A Case of You" in its final form. Is the rhyme scheme AABB ("said/said/dark[ness]/bar")? Or are the rhymes "Lost/star/dark[ness]/bar"? And if it's the latter, does that equal ABCB, or should the rhyme scheme be notated as ABBB? To complicate matters, there are the internal rhymes of "got," "lost," "constant," "constantly" and "want." That most of these rhymes hit the ear only subliminally is the point. It shouldn't be clear—affairs of the heart, like "A Case of You" and the songs Joni wrote after, rarely move in neat, easy lines. You have to read between them.

In *Claims for Poetry*, the poet Donald Hall writes, "Meter is nothing but a loose set of probabilities; it is a trick easily learned... But only when you have forgotten the requirements of meter do you begin to write poetry in it." Emily Dickinson put it another way: "Tell the truth, but tell it slant." Undeniably a great song, "A Case of You" is also great poetry.

But as I said, and to contradict myself a little, none of this really mattered when I first heard "A Case of You" in Wally's apartment eighteen years ago—and to be honest, it still doesn't really. I just loved it. It's certainly true that the lyric does what any great work should do, filling the senses on first encounter and revealing deeper meaning each time it's revisited. But all those deeper readings were only possible because the music—of the dulcimer, of Joni's voice, of the poetry—were so captivating that I've wanted to revisit it over the years. It presents itself to the listener as a fully realized being—body, bones, blood, flesh; it can be understood sensually on first listen—one person's inside speaking to another person's inside. It can be absorbed into the body while the intellect is still catching up.

William Faulkner famously wrote, "In writing, you must kill your darlings"—a reminder to writers that they mustn't let their favorite lines or pet phrases get in the way of the story they want to tell. Joni Mitchell has similarly said, "The lines that matter most in my songs are the ones I leave out."

Perhaps a future version of this essay will take a cue from these two great writers and be more to the point. It will read, in total: "I just love it."

THE LAST TIME I SAW RICHARD

The last time I saw Richard
Was Detroit in '68 and he told me,
"All romantics meet the same fate,
Someday...
Cynical and drunk
And boring someone in some dark café
You laugh," he said
"You think you're immune...
Go look at your eyes...
They're two blue moons
You like roses
And kisses
And pretty men to tell you pretty lies"

"Pretty Lies
When're you going to realize
They're only pretty lies
Just pretty lies
Pretty Lies"

He put a quarter in the Wurlitzer
And he pushed
Three buttons
And the thing began to whirr
And a bar maid came by
In fishnet stockings and a bow tie
And she said "Drink up now it's gettin' on time to close"
"Richard, you haven't really changed" I said
"It's just that now you're romanticizing some pain that's in your head
You got tombs in your eyes
But the songs you punched are dreamy
Listen—they talk of love so sweet"

"Love so sweet
When're you gonna get yourself back on your feet?
Oh love can be so sweet
Love is so sweet"

Richard got married to a figure skater
And he bought her a dishwasher
And a coffee percolator
And he drinks at home now most nights with the TV on
And all the house lights left up bright
I'm gonna blow this damn candle out
I don't want nobody comin' over to my table
I got nothing to talk to anybody about
All good dreamers pass this way
Someday
Hidin' behind bottles
In dark cafes

Dark cafés
Only a dark cocoon before I get my gorgeous wings and fly away
Only a phase
These
Dark
Café
Days

THE LAST TIME I SAW RICHARD

KIM ADDONIZIO

I'm on a United flight from Oakland to New York; I'm having a second glass of chardonnay because I like to drink on planes, because this morning began terribly, because I recently went through another breakup and am alone. Because I sometimes imagine, not in a positive way, being alone for the next several years of nights. "The Last Time I Saw Richard" is running through my head; I'm thinking about the choices we make, domesticity and freedom, Richard drinking in front of the TV and the song's speaker in a dark café not wholly convincing herself that this part of her life is prelude, only temporary.

Who the Richard of the song is, we never quite know. An old lover. A once-friend whose dreams erode in suburbia just as Frank and April Wheeler's do in *Revolutionary Road*:

> Richard got married to a figure skater
> And he bought her a dishwasher
> And a coffee percolator
> And he drinks at home now most nights with the TV on
> And all the house lights left up bright

But it's the speaker I most connect with in the song, the woman who is consumed with the possibilities and failures of romantic love, her eyes "full of moon."

Like every other adolescent girl I knew, I played the album *Blue* over and over, and quickly knew all the lyrics by heart. And by whatever is deeper than the heart—the foul rag and bone shop, the dirt and earth and darkness beneath that. "Acid, booze, and ass / Needles, guns, and grass." Some of these I had yet to experience, but I felt I understood something of their siren call. I wore my hair long and parted in the middle, convinced I was destined to become another Joni, to perform songs I had not yet written on the nylon string guitar I couldn't yet play very well. At nineteen, having dropped out of college, I spent some time in L.A., staying in a friend's studio apartment, living on one large chocolate-chip cookie and a can of apricot nectar a day. The friend went to work in a bank, and I stayed in and worked on my songs, listening to the couple next door scream; I mean, full-on, insanely scream—they were in Primal Therapy. Occasionally I splurged on coffee and cheesecake in a café on Sunset Boulevard where *Court and Spark* seemed to play continuously and where I was sure it was obvious to everyone that I was too poor and uncool to belong. I gave myself until the age of twenty-five to make it as a singer, whatever that meant to me at the time. Six years seemed a long apprenticeship.

To look clearly at the world and render it in words is so difficult. Even more difficult to make those words sound simple and inevitable.

> He put a quarter in the Wurlitzer
> And he pushed
> Three buttons
> And the thing began to whirr
> And a bar maid came by
> In fishnet stockings and a bow tie
> And she said "Drink up now it's getting on time to close"

That's as precise and natural as it gets.

Dark cafés in San Francisco: I was twenty-something, like every other person I knew—if there were older people we didn't see them, they existed in some other realm, at the periphery of our vision, and we never turned our heads. We were fry cooks, waitresses, office clerks, jewelry makers. We were beers, screwdrivers, margaritas on the rocks, no salt. Often, cheap wine. Nights at the Sixteenth Note, we played pool and drank. I would get wasted and meet boys and go home with them. I'd never see them again.

After music, poetry struck me in my late twenties with a force that nearly stunned me, and I apprenticed myself to it and to the life of a writer. Without Joni's songs—songs that had found their way into me at a young age—I'm not sure I would have known how or where to begin. Begin here, her words said. With the self and its struggles. With sorrow and confusion and loneliness. Don't leave out the joy, either. That is: tell the truth about life.

> I'm gonna blow this damn candle out
> I don't want nobody comin' over to my table
> I got nothing to talk to anybody about

> Tennessee Williams in *The Glass Menagerie*: "Blow out your candles, Laura." The Gentleman Caller engaged to another girl, the fragile fantastic unicorn in pieces on the floor.

It's those lines in the song I think I love most: their scorching honesty, the turn from the glaring lights in Richard's house to the candle in the café that becomes the small flame of hope in the speaker, a mocking promise, one that possibly won't be kept. Better to extinguish that hope? In the end, the woman in the café tells herself, "Only a phase, these dark café days." She may yet get her wings. Or she may find herself sitting there, or a place very much like it, thirty years on.

When I was young—when my parents would never die and I would never meet anyone to love, when the Vietnam War would never end no matter how many people marched in the streets—I listened, like everyone else I knew, to a lot of singer-songwriters. It felt as though the world we had inherited was about to split open, to reveal the flowering of consciousness. "We are stardust, we are golden." We were going to get back to the garden. It has proved otherwise. Still I can't help thinking of what Brecht wrote: "In a dark time, will there be singing? / Yes, there will be singing. About the dark time."

For me, Joan Baez was Joan Baez, Bob Dylan was Dylan, but Joni Mitchell was always Joni. When I was seventeen, she was the angel in my ear. "You're in my blood like holy wine... I am on a lonely road and I am traveling." She knew me even before I knew myself; it was that personal. And it still is.

BANQUET

Come to the dinner gong
The table is laden high
Fat bellies and hungry little ones
Tuck your napkins in
And take your share
Some get the gravy
And some get the gristle
Some get the marrow bone
And some get nothing
Though there's plenty to spare
I took my share down by the sea
Paper plates and Javex bottles on the tide
Seagulls come down
And they squawk at me
Down where the water skiers glide

Some turn to Jesus
And some turn to heroin
Some turn to rambling round
Looking for a clean sky
And a drinking stream
Some watch the paint peel off
Some watch their kids grow up
Some watch their stocks and bonds
Waiting for that big deal
American Dream
I took my dream down by the sea
Yankee yachts and lobster pots and sunshine
And logs and sails
And Shell Oil pails
Dogs and tugs and summertime
Back in the banquet line
Angry young people crying

Who let the greedy in
And who left the needy out
Who made this salty soup
Tell him we're very hungry now
For a sweeter fare
In the cookie I read
"Some get the gravy
And some get the gristle
Some get the marrow bone
And some get nothing
Though there's plenty to spare"

WINTER 1972

ANJANI THOMAS

Banquet
Cold Blue Steel And Sweet Fire
Barangrill

I dropped the diamond needle on those three tracks again and again
unable to go further...
my twelve-year-old mind struggling to break Joni's code.

First, the voice...
light as silk thread
woven over and under open tunings
pulled taut through a chain of vibey piano chords
and wound through songs so mysterious
I could barely penetrate the heartrending messages they carried.

This wasn't earthy Joan or sweet Judy or comfortable Carole...
no, this woman danced on the raw edge of almost—
never too hungry
or obvious—
she entertained herself with a guitar and a pack of cigarettes
and didn't mind if you joined the party or not.
And she did not give a damn about the rules of songwriting.
Where were the common rhymes and scans?
Chorus hooks?
Even her background vocals were oddly shaped
clusters of bittersweet dissonance... and I was captivated.

Joni was too wild to anticipate let alone imitate.
I wanted to get her—
hell, I wanted to be her—

but I never could
because truth be told
she kinda scared me.
For as much as she knew the mysteries of love
and the inner secrets of daisies and poets
and as often as she—
intimate companion of fierce wind and feral trees—
divined the anthems that soothe a wounded female's heart...
she navigated a world of shady bars and distant dreams
with junkies exhaling the stale air of defeat...
shipwrecked souls
and live wires
littered beaches
forest fires...
mourning the dead end of a rich repast
and the final judgment of moon and stars.

Her long-legged beauty made you want to chase after her
but Joni asked a lot of a listener... even one with trained ears.
Hep cats ripped through every #5 and m9th at Main Street and Cotton Avenue
but record execs nipped at her heels, barking,
No art songs! Make another *Court and Spark*!
Joni wasn't about to turn around and head back.
She figured the suits would sell it and the crowd would catch up sooner or later.
But not everyone made it.
Some stayed ashore,
listening for her bell tones every now and then from the safety of their armchairs.
Some rippled the surfaces, playing guitar and singing the early songs for friends,
appreciating what came later with a by now educated ear... courtesy of Joni.
And a few like Mingus and Jaco
met her laughing in the whirlpools...
churning
curving
blowing bars of jazz and gold
in the ocean light.

Banquet
Cold Blue Steel And Sweet Fire
Barangrill

Listening to them now, I think,
Has it really been forty years?
Her melodies are pure and striking as ever
But the memories I tied to those songs are fading under the collapse of time.
I've learned to forgive the fool, the liar, the betrayer and my beloved...
so I understand why,
realizing that so few get it—
Joni retreated to her lair.
I pray she has found peace in the uneasy truce
but who knows what opus we lost in the course of her moving on.

These days I imagine her painting, much the way she used to sing.
Drawing her brush right past the borders of sterile white canvas...
saturating walls and mirrors and lampposts with wet strokes of lament
Laurel Canyon greens and grey smoke
daubs of beauty
dark reality
and a trace of blonde regret.

The three songs I reference in particular are inextricably woven together in my mind. Not only was each one a jewel of lyrical depth, vocal beauty, and melodic and theoretical complexity, but when she played piano or guitar, Joni made it sound so effortless that only an accomplished musician would know how challenging it really was to duplicate. As a visionary artist, poet and musical innovator, Joni has inspired so many—including me—to pursue the path of a singer-songwriter, and she remains a beacon for us all.

FOR THE ROSES

I heard it in the wind last night
It sounded like applause
Did you get a round resounding for you way up here?
It seems like many dim years ago
Since I heard that face to face
Or seen you face to face
Though tonight I can feel you here
I get these notes
On butterflies and lilac sprays
From girls who just have to tell me
That they saw you somewhere...

In some office sits a poet
And he trembles as he sings
And he asks some guy
To circulate his soul around
On your mark red ribbon runner
The caressing rev of motors
Finely tuned like fancy women
In thirties evening gowns
Up the charts
Off to the airport
Your name's in the news
Everything's first class
And the lights go down
And it's just you up there
Getting them to feel like that...

Remember the days when you used to sit
And make up your tunes for love
And pour your simple sorrow
To the soundhole and your knee
And now you're seen
On giant screens
And at parties for the press
And for people who have slices of you
From the company
They toss around your latest golden egg
Speculation—well, who's to know
If the next one in the nest
Will glitter for them so...

I guess I seem ungrateful
With my teeth sunk in the hand
That brings me these things
I really can't give up just yet
Now I sit up here
The critic!
And they introduce some band
But they seem so much confetti
Looking at them on my TV set
Oh the power and the glory
Just when you're getting a taste for worship
They start bringing out the hammers
And the boards
And the nails

I heard it in the wind last night
It sounded like applause
Chilly now
End of summer
No more shiny hot nights
It was just the arbutus rustling
And the bumping of the logs
And the moon swept down black water
Like an empty spotlight...

THREE POEMS INSPIRED BY "FOR THE ROSES"

LYN LIFSHIN

I think of her watching the
last rose petals on a
day like today, say deep
August, browning like
an old rubber doll
she might have left
in an attic in Canada.
I think of her pressing
skin against glass, a sense
of summertime falling,
that sense of fall
that that Sylvia Plath
wrote of. Or maybe some
freeze frame of what
is going, moving on.
I see her pale arms,
sea mist velvet jeans
hugging hips that
never will not be boyish.
In the wind, gone
voices move close
to her cheek bones. In
this frame she could be in
a fancy 30s gown. Some
thing is raw, some thing
is broken. It has to be
a full moon
etching black water.
She has to know that
from what is torn
and scarred, some

thing almost too
exquisitely beautiful
is already stirring,
something dark
as coal becoming
diamond, insistent,
dying to be born

Sometimes I think of her
as a wild foal, hardly
touching down in prairie
grass, Saskatchewan. Or a
sea nymph, her gaze
glued to the deepest
emerald wave, a Silkie
luring men she can't stay
with long. There she
is, on a seaweed jeweled
rock, her songs, ribbons
of melancholy lassoing you,
pulling on your heart.
Some say Bessie Smith
left even or especially good
men to have something
to make her songs
burn the hottest blues. I
think of Joni knowing
what can't stay, what is so
broken it catches the
light like torn bottles
the ocean's turned
to sea glass jewels, that
what dissolves
behind you in the rear
view mirror haunts,

knife-like as her trees,
slashes of wild paint
shivering in a naked row,
such exquisite beauty
in wreckage

I wore Tea Rose and
often a black rose
in my hair that summer,
symbol of freedom,
a nod to the White Rose,
the German girl who
protesting the Nazis,
gave her skin, her lips
and heart, her life. I was
flying coast to coast
to read, coming back
to an alone house. Named
for the rose, for a aunt
adventurous as Joni,
who danced in flames,
I dressed in rose. Deborah
of the roses. The stories
about her whispered by
grown-ups behind stained
glass doors. Who wouldn't
expect roses in my poems?
White rose, Bulgarian
rose. When I walked thru
airports with a white
rose from Allen Ginsberg
everyone whispered, "roses."
But it was the rose scent
perfuming the air from my
body. You could almost

hear, as even now I can
almost feel the one who
touched me on that
coast, what Joni heard
in the wind, the end
of, the chilly now,
the last face to face

It had to be in the mid-'70s when, just divorced, my blues echoed what I imagined Joni Mitchell's to be. I just have stacks of her 33s, slightly musty, covers frayed in a little in a house I'm rarely in. I think of myself still in those rooms, waiting for a lover to drive up. It's like a museum—a freeze frame—the way poems and songs, especially Joni's, can be: a nostalgic, sadly gorgeous sliver of what isn't, was or maybe couldn't be.

I selected to write about Joni's song "For the Roses" for many reasons. I love the record jacket, where she is wearing velvet and boots, as I so often did and do. We both paint, as reclusive a choice as writing. I too started as an art major, was sure that would be what I needed to do. I love her drawing. I feel a kinship in terms of our words, our images: her songs are clearly poems, suggestive and magical with enough left out. The leaps, like in all blues, are something I feel is a quality in my own work. There are leaps in all blues, and I use them in my work as well. I so often love what's left out, and if I find too much is there, I try to change it. The cadence, the sensuality, the juxtaposition of nature and emotion, such strong images like "And the moon swept down black water / Like an empty spotlight...." Lyrical, mysterious—just lovely. Poetry, definitely.

"Rose" suggests so many things to me: the roses at Churchill Downs for the Kentucky Derby, the last rose of summer, "Abby's Irish Rose," the blood of Christ, the ballet *Specter of the Rose*, the sensual roses of the body.

Of course all flowers die, but somehow the dying rose seems to have that mix of excruciating beauty and then its loss. I can remember my first corsage: a yellow rose.

Every part of this song connects to some freeze frame in my life, and makes me remember things I hadn't thought of in years. Vividly as the smell of the roses, I'm drawn to how Joni writes of what can't stay, but also of the beauty that comes from this, the fierceness. Trieste and joy—as if the joy depends on what dark things one has gone through.

JUDGEMENT OF THE MOON AND STARS

No tongue in the bell
And the fishwives yell
But they might as well be mute
So you get to keep the pictures—
That don't seem like much!
Cold white keys under your fingers
Now you're thinking
"That's no substitute
It just don't do it
Like the song of a warm warm body
Loving your touch"

In the court they carve your legend
With an apple in its jaw
And the women that you wanted
They get their laughs
Long silk stockings
On the bedposts of refinement
You're too raw
They think you're too raw
It's the judgement of the moon and stars
Your solitary path
Draw yourself a bath
Think what you'd like to have
For supper
Or take a walk
A park
A bridge
A tree
A river
Revoked but not yet cancelled
The gift goes on

In silence
In a bell jar
Still the song

You've got to shake your fists at lightning now
You've got to roar like forest fire
You've got to spread your light like blazes
All across the sky
They're going to aim the hoses on you
Show 'em you won't expire
Not till you burn up every passion
Not even when you die
Come on now
You've got to try
If you're feeling contempt
Well then you tell it
If you're tired of the silent night
Jesus, well then you yell it
Condemned to wires and hammers
Strike every chord that you feel
That broken trees
And elephant ivories
Conceal

CONFLUENCE

LISA SORNBERGER

Tonight feels different. It is an exceptionally mild February night here in Connecticut, and a full moon illumines the sky. Snow Moon, Hunger Moon, Opening Buds Moon are the beautiful and apt Native American names for this moon. They resonate with the state of mind I'm in.

I've gone out into the bright winter night to move fully into the present. I release myself from old sorrows and stasis, and feel my spirit and creative energy free up.

I head to my writing room, to get to the heart of my piece for this book. I listen to Joni, as I have countless other times over the past thirty-seven years, to help propel me deeper into my own creative state; that spacious place all poets and artists long for. It feels like home. Tonight I am playing "Judgement of The Moon and Stars" and "Turbulent Indigo," and thinking of Beethoven, Van Gogh and Joni.

Joni has always written with unflinching honesty, courage, and integrity to her own vision. She has a painter's precise eye for visual images and a poet's ear that translates her visions and feelings into stunningly artful language. She hears the way both poets and musicians do—rhyme, rhythm, metrics—and has the poet's gift for metaphor.

She tells the human condition, and it doesn't matter whether her words are autobiographical, fictional, political, societal... or not; they resonate so powerfully with so many of us, and give us a deeper understanding of our own lives, and of Life.

I have listened to Joni since I was fifteen. My mother remembers my playing Joni's music constantly throughout high school, writing my own poems and trying to draw pictures like Joni's on the walls of my bedroom. My stepmother, who loved "Both Sides Now," recalls giving me a Christmas gift that she believes was *Clouds*, my first Joni album, in 1974. I am not sure if it was this album, or *Court and Spark*, or a friend playing one of Joni's songs on the guitar that brought me to her. Regardless, once I found her words, I would never leave. My friends and I shared our love of all things Joni. I wrote a high school paper titled "Joni Mitchell: Portrait of a Poet and a Painter." At the very least, a fifteen-year-old girl and her astute teacher got that Joni was more than just a singer-songwriter.

Linda remembers our carrying on conversations that consisted of lines of Joni's poetry. Paula handwrote me a copy of "Marcie" with the most basic chords. Terry and I hung out in parks with our guitars—carried more for show than playing, at least in my case. Sue, another Mitchell devotee, much later named her son "Mitchell" in honor of Joni. Marsha made her little sister learn and recite Joni songs for some reason! Later in life, Sandy and I shared our love of Joni's work, and our painting and poetry forged a bond. Her paintings sometimes sparked my poems, and my poems her paintings. Jill and I shared music and poetry, and are happily doing so once again, our conversations full of Joni. There was fun, wildness and, for some of us, difficulty and unspoken sorrow beyond the teenaged norm, as Jill alludes to in "A Thread of Joni" in this book. Some of my memories from those days are sketchy from constant stress. But some of my happiest recollections are of sitting next to the stereo, my ear brushing the woven fabric face of the cabinet that housed the turntable, controls and speakers. Basking in Joni's words and music, taking in her album cover art while reading her words, each album was a singular, gorgeous book of poems, hot off the press. Joni's words were a both a refuge and an affirmation, somehow, that we were all okay, and that we would find our own way in the world. In a time of great transition for women in our society, she showed by example that we were free to choose our own paths, even if they were somewhat unconventional.

I'd wanted to be a writer since the age of nine, started writing poems at fourteen, and here was a brilliant, dynamic woman affirming the path of the poet rather than life in the domestic or corporate worlds that appeared to be the logical choices, the ones that would please others. My family did support my pursuit of poetry, but encouraged me to go to college, major in liberal arts and, somehow, prepare for a career. Write poetry but "don't quit your day job."

I remember vividly the kindness of a family friend named Ed Rathke, whose generous gift of a twenty-five dollar gift certificate to the coolest record store in Hartford allowed me to purchase *For The Roses* in 1975, along with three other albums. And what an album it was! Real poetry. I loved poetry: the Beat poets (especially Ferlinghetti and Snyder), Sylvia Plath, Erica Jong, among others. Then there were the singer-songwriters I sometimes thought of as poets. Joni was, though, and always will be, in a category of her own. She is the one I listen to all the time, whose words I know by heart.

For the Roses was a revelation—akin to nothing I'd ever heard or read before.

The follow-up to *Blue*, the favorite of many of Joni's fans, *Roses*, like *Blue* was groundbreaking in its openness. It is emotionally honest, rich with introspection and "digs down deep" into personal and universal truths. It is infused with wisdom and feeling, yet… tempered by a little distance and coolness on many levels. It has a quality of passionate detachment. *Roses* was made primarily at Joni's cabin-home in British Columbia, where she had headed, as I understand it, to take time out from L.A., the music scene, huge successes, pressures, disappointments in work and love. She'd gone due north to her cabin in the woods by the Pacific Ocean, it seems, to reground and heal herself.

I find it telling and relevant that she chose a picture of herself naked to put inside the album cover. Seen only from the back, while standing firmly footed on a rock, she reveals her most private self to herself and the open sea. This picture and these poems are of both rock and ocean, solid and fluid. Born in solitude, they embrace coming home and finding balance after tumult. The results are exquisite.

"Judgement of the Moon and Stars" is a masterpiece; an achingly beautiful, tender yet tough "talk" to Beethoven, with whom I imagine Joni felt a kinship. In a concert in 1972, Joni said the song came to her after reading a book about Beethoven's spirituality, which I believe to be *Beethoven's Spiritual Search*, by JNM Sullivan. She said she wrote this as an attempt to encourage him ("Too late," she chuckled), to shake off his depression.

Joni brings levity into her introduction with her sense of humor, but the song itself is anything but light. In her straightforward and strikingly poetic way, she writes with astute observation, succinct language, bright imagery, fresh metaphor. Her lines and images here are stark, eloquent, direct and elegant: both minimalist and complex, same as her accompanying music. Her expressed emotions are poignant and fiery, yet cooled by her solo voice and piano. There is empathy in her words and voice. There is a loneliness conveyed by that solo piano and by Joni's singing her own harmonies. The effect is deeply moving, never sentimental.

In describing Beethoven's experience as imaginatively and intimately as if it were her own, Joni accomplishes what I believe fine art is meant to do. When a writer or painter or composer addresses and conjures the personal (her own or someone else's, even a fictionalized reality), she essentially allows us to enter our own experience more deeply. In "Judgement," she speaks about the historical and imagined experience of the brilliant composer with deep sensitivity and intuition. Exploring the frontier of music, painting, knowledge and self-knowledge requires courage. Beethoven's lonely spiritual dilemma clearly seemed to touch her. He was a recognized genius, yet never fully in favor at court. Light years ahead of his contemporaries, he was highly acknowledged, yet underwent great disappointments in his career, love and life. He struggled with ill health and suffered the ultimate insult: the loss of his hearing. Still, he not only endured, but continued to create at an even more profound level. He created some of his best music after becoming deaf, including his "Ninth Symphony," considered by many music critics to be one of his best—if not his best! He held onto Art as a path to enlightenment.

To greater and lesser degrees, all artists and others who are blessed with vision and intuition beyond the norm have both a gift and the burden of carrying it in a world that doesn't affirm these realms as much as others. Joni's poem addresses the fact that each of us is ultimately alone and must be self-reliant and cling to our creativity—not only to survive, but also to thrive. She shines a light on a solo, but shared, journey.

On to a more specific analysis of "Judgment of the Moon and Stars," stanza by stanza:

No tongue in the bell
And the fishwives yell
But they might as well be mute
So you get to keep the pictures—
That don't seem like much!
Cold white keys under your fingers
Now you're thinking
"That's no substitute
It just don't do it
Like the song of a warm warm body
Loving your touch"

Here are visceral, earthy visual images for speech—tongue,
and yelling fishwives
Sound and silence—
Then a switch to a visual, cold world,
from a warm and sensual
kinesthetic/auditory one.

In the court they carve your legend
With an apple in its jaw
And the women that you wanted
They get their laughs
Long silk stockings
On the bedposts of refinement
You're too raw
They think you're too raw
It's the judgement of the moon and stars
Your solitary path
Draw yourself a bath
Think what you'd like to have
For supper
Or take a walk
A park
A bridge
A tree
A river
Revoked but not yet cancelled
The gift goes on

The artist gets praise and prizes,
but is not fully understood—
relegated to an idea, a legend.
He is unable to stay with his true loves...
(In Beethoven's case, unable to marry,
as he was not of their social station)
There is the coldness of the infinite sky
His path—Aloneness
Her advice: Warm yourself,
feed yourself,
move...
ground on the path—
take in this list of seen things,
moment to moment
Then, a turn, as in a sonnet...
Ah—the gift may be temporarily taken,
but it isn't gone...
The artist may be deaf,
But he still has his genius,
his music...

In silence
In a bell jar
Still the song

You've got to shake your fists at lightning now
You've got to roar like forest fire
You've got to spread your light like blazes
All across the sky
They're going to aim the hoses on you
Show 'em you won't expire
Not till you burn up every passion
Not even when you die
Come on now
You've got to try
If you're feeling contempt
Well then you tell it
If you're tired of the silent night
Jesus, well then you yell it
Condemned to wires and hammers
Strike every chord that you feel
That broken trees
And elephant ivories
Conceal

Her advice: take very physical actions. Shake your fists at the sky, at the lightning strike (of God? Fate?) Project into the silent, visual world with the voice of a lion. Light the night sky on fire (like Van Gogh?) They will try to extinguish your passion but cannot if you won't allow it. Speak your anger! Shout your sorrow! Art is your path—indestructible, imperative. The piano itself, interestingly, is described in visual and visceral images (none auditory) of broken things—cut trees and killed animals. Very poignant and effective ways to conjure silence, and exquisite as a metaphor for the genius himself. The instrument is made by destruction. The exterior holds and guards the gift—the music and the heart of the genius—intact and vibrant.

I repeatedly come back to this song to remind myself of many things: to return to myself, to nurture my spirit, to remember that creativity is the antidote to depression. Passion, Art and yelling in the night when the night gets dark: these are the things that get us through. Erica Jong once said that everyone has talent, but few have the willingness to go to the dark place it leads them. Blessings to all of us, as we each follow our own way through the dark to the light.

CONFLUENCE (for Joni Mitchell)

A river runs through a forest,
comes to a clearing,
where sun streams through trees.

Deep springs feed into streams
flow into one another lose themselves
become one water.

Raven, fox, bear...
my totem animals called me here.
They spoke in my dreams

whispered true words
that entered unfiltered
to wake me from sleep.

I followed the raven here,
listened to my Muse
trusted her to take me

to this place beyond harm,
where light sifts through trees,
warms skin, fur, and feather.

Spirit Bear gather here,
dip powerful paws
deep into the river.

Salmon swim uphill forever
all their lives,
just to get here.

Birds abound around us,
light and song are falling and flying,
and each of us, all are singing.

Thank you, Joni, for gracing our lives with your gifts.

COURT AND SPARK

Love came to my door
With a sleeping roll
And a madman's soul
He thought for sure I'd seen him
Dancing up a river in the dark
Looking for a woman
To court and spark

He was playing on the sidewalk
For passing change
When something strange happened
Glory train passed through him
So he buried the coins he made
In People's Park
And went looking for a woman
To court and spark

It seemed like he read my mind
He saw me mistrusting him
And still acting kind
He saw how I worried sometimes
I worry sometimes

"All the guilty people" he said
They've all seen the stain
On their daily bread
On their Christian names
I cleared myself
I sacrificed my blues
And you could complete me
I'd complete you

His eyes were the color of the sand
And the sea
And the more he talked to me
The more he reached me
But I couldn't let go of L.A.
City of the fallen angels

THE PORTAL AND THE LANGUAGE

STEVEN ALBAHARI

Music serves as a bookmark for times gone past. Like photographs, songs pull shape, form, and color from our memory and help us to recreate the connection with past events of our lives. Each of us gravitates toward music which helps to acknowledge and create our reflections in the world and serve as landmarks for our interpretations. And while they may change, our interpretations are what define the quality of our experience then and now. What was once is not now and what is now will never be again. But the songs that bring our memories back validate that we are alive. They remind us that we were relevant then and that we are relevant now.

While we court the people and events in our lives to become part of the yet unwritten script for them, we have no choice but to improvise to get there. To improvise is a worthy endeavor because from it we can become receptive through listening and responsive through understanding. Through it we find a spark that may help us make sense of things. Music is the portal while poetry is the language.

Musicians and poets help us define our lives and it is seemingly rare when we find in the music real poetry that helps us define our lives and take us to places of purpose, places we want to return to and long to be, places where we are transformed. Transformed not just then, but now, as well. That is the magic which happens when music and real poetry come together. This synergy seems rare, but not in the magic of Joni Mitchell.

Joni helps us find the door and then gently leads us to our own reflections. With angels standing by, she courts us with an invitation to live and to love.

HELP ME

Help me
I think I'm falling
In love again
When I get that crazy feeling
I know
I'm in trouble again!
I'm in trouble
'Cause you're a rambler and a gambler
And a sweet talking ladies man
And you love your lovin'
But not like you love your freedom

Help me
I think I'm falling
In love too fast
It's got me hoping for the future
And worrying about the past
'Cause I've seen some hot hot blazes
Come down to smoke and ash
We love our lovin'
But not like we love our freedom

Didn't it feel good
We were sitting there talking
Or lying there not talking
Didn't it feel good
To dance with the lady
With the hole in her stocking
Didn't it feel good
Didn't it feel good

Help me
I think I'm falling
In love with you
Are you going to let me go there by myself?
That's such a lonely thing to do
Both of us flirting around
Flirting and flirting
Hurting too
We love our lovin'
But not like we love our freedom

THE BEGUINE

COLEEN J. McELROY

a woman walks into a room
a man catches her eye
you know the story...
the slow dance as they circle
each other in guileless moves
or so it seems
the old crisscross of heel and toe
the old dance that lovers do

the old razzmatazz
the dizzying spin
that leaves them breathless...
together they are perfect
when he reels her in
she is his lamb forever
and he is her soul-mate
before they take one last
breath and step away
before the story takes hold

one turn and the contact
so accidental both are left
gasping in the what went
wrong of it all
both left erasing air
of any trace of what they knew
must have been there
had to have been there
before they even knew
they were looking for it...

From the very first time I listened to Joni Mitchell's rendition of "Help Me," I was struck by the way the words commanded the music. The song was a cautionary tale but with a light hearted melody that helped me imagine dancers spinning around the floor, their feet barely touching down before the next step. You sense the humor and pathos in her poetry, and hear the way the music dovetails with a shift in tempo. Having been a dancer, many decades ago, I heard the foxtrot, a pattern that can make even competitive dancers uneasy. The slightest misstep and the partners are left, like lovers, trying to regain their footing. "Help Me" captures the hesitation of yielding to the dance, and to love—the excitement at first, then the hope that you can get through it all unscathed.

I wanted to capture the plaintive quality of Mitchell's poetry—straightforward and unadorned with the superlatives of metaphors, yet embellished with an honesty that suggests fingers lightly touching a keyboard. I concentrated on a lilting melody that, like the foxtrot, gives way to a faster rhythm. Mitchell's poetic patterns follow this perfectly. As the smooth flowing movements change, syllabics multiply, and her voice gains an edginess, almost a Latin beat, the flourish of arpeggios ending with the harmonious "we"—both partners becoming culpable in this dance. Joni Mitchell's songs have stayed with me over the years, unaccompanied, as with her lyrics, by ultra-technology. Just hum a few bars, and I'll do the rest.

FREE MAN IN PARIS

"The way I see it," he said
"You just can't win it
Everybody's in it for their own gain
You can't please 'em all
There's always somebody calling you down
I do my best
And I do good business
There's a lot of people asking for my time
They're trying to get ahead
They're trying to be a good friend of mine

I was a free man in Paris
I felt unfettered and alive
There was nobody calling me up for favors
And no one's future to decide...
You know I'd go back there tomorrow
But for the work I've taken on—
Stoking the star maker machinery
Behind the popular song

I deal in dreamers
And telephone screamers
Lately I wonder what I do it for
If l had my way
I'd just walk through those doors
And wander
Down the Champs Elysées
Going café to cabaret
Thinking how I'll feel when I find
That very good friend of mine

I was a free man in Paris
I felt unfettered and alive
Nobody was calling me up for favors
No one's future to decide
You know I'd go back there tomorrow
But for the work I've taken on
Stoking the star maker machinery
Behind the popular song"

SPEAKING WITH DAVID GEFFEN REGARDING "FREE MAN IN PARIS"

LISA SORNBERGER

David Geffen is both extremely busy and very private. Who could blame him? He must be bombarded with requests twenty-four-seven. No one needs me to fill them in on his amazing career as record label owner turned film producer turned philanthropist. David created Asylum and Geffen Records, then, with Steven Spielberg and Jeffrey Katzenberg, created DreamWorks Studios and, at the time, made the single largest unrestricted donation to a medical university—now the David Geffen School of Medicine at UCLA.

Geffen has a gift for recognizing serious talent, and it is fair to say that he helped shape and define the musical taste and culture of a generation or two, then moved on to become an equally brilliant philanthropist.

Therefore, I feel very lucky to have had a few minutes on the phone with him to facilitate his contribution to this book on Joni's poetry. He is not without humor, but clearly doesn't waste time or words, nor bother to be indirect. He made it most clear that he would not be talking with me were it not for Joni. Fair enough. Clearly, the fact that Joni wants him included in the project matters to him.

There's an irony in approaching the man bombarded with non-stop requests with... a request, particularly one for him to speak about "Free Man in Paris," in which Joni wrote, of all the requests of him, "there's a lot of people asking for my time, they're trying to get ahead, they're trying to be a good friend of mine." Yes, here I was, another stranger at the doorstep who wanted something. The difference here, though, was that he'd responded to my invitation to join in this book *for Joni*.

"Free Man in Paris," for the purposes of this book, seemed the logical choice of songs to talk about, as it was written about him. About him, not for him, he dryly pointed out to me. I also wanted him to express whatever else he might want to say about Joni, as we honored her creative genius.

Regarding "Free Man in Paris," he explained that he and Joni were in Paris with Robbie Robertson and his wife when Joni wrote the song.

There was something genuinely moving about hearing this powerful man who is, by necessity, guarded and clearly not interested in small talk with a stranger, say, "I love the song, and I love Joni." Simply stated, eloquent and obviously true.

I asked what else he might want to say to her in the book, and he replied that she is his favorite artist from his entire career and the greatest songwriter/poet from the second half of the twentieth century.

Additionally, I asked if Joni's creative process sparked his own and vice versa, and he said that Joni made her albums entirely herself, writing, producing, et cetera, stating in no uncertain terms that it was "like they were there to deliver her baby."

After our talk, which took me a bit off-guard, I gathered my thoughts, and his, as quickly as I could so as not to lose content or intent. Then I called his assistant, Serina, to thank her for facilitating our meeting.

I told her I felt like a tornado had just blown through my office. She understood, and said, "Yes, it's great, isn't it, how he does that?"

Indeed it is.

With thanks to David Geffen and Serina Tremayne

TROUBLE CHILD

Up in a sterilized room
Where they let you be lazy
Knowing your attitude's all wrong
And you've got to change
And that's not easy
Dragon shining with all values known
Dazzling you
Keeping you from your own
Where is the lion in you to defy him
When you're this weak
And this spacey?

So what are you going to do about it
You can't live life and you can't leave it
Advice and religion
You can't take it
You can't seem to believe it
The peacock is afraid to parade
You're under the thumb of the maid
You really can't give love in this condition
Still you know how you need it

They open and close you
Then they talk like they know you
They don't know you
They're friends and they're foes too
Trouble child
Breaking like the waves at Malibu

So why does it come as such a shock

To know you really have no one

Only a river of changing faces

Looking for an ocean

They trickle through your leaky plans

Another dream over the dam

And you're lying in some room

Feeling like your right to be human

Is going over too

Well some are going to knock you

And some'll try to clock you

You know it's really hard

To talk sense to you

Trouble child

Breaking like the waves at Malibu

TROUBLE CHILD

STEVE STARGER

I.

"Breaking like the waves at Malibu"
Malibu is twenty-two miles from Laurel Canyon. Fort MacLeod, AB, Canada, is 1,445 miles from Hollywood, California. Lots of busking and bars, fame and notoriety in between for the Lady of the Canyon.

"Breaking like the waves at Malibu"

Malibu, the ultimate Southern California playground of the rich and famous, and surfers and wannabes who hold down three jobs to scrounge a driver's license with a Malibu address—your ticket to Paradise—promising endless mauve sunsets; sleek, languid women in bikinis and flowing designer robes; the finest wine; the finest dope (Steely Dan, "Hey Nineteen"—"The Cuervo Gold / the fine Columbian / make tonight / a wonderful thing"). What an apt metaphor—an exquisite shank to the heart, especially if you've seen the waves break at Malibu—beautiful and deadly.

"Dragon shining with all values known / Dazzling you / Keeping you from your own"

"Dragon" in one definition is street talk for heroin. If I apply this definition, I think of "Cold Blue Steel and Sweet Fire," and Steely Dan, from "Time Out of Mind": "Tonight when I chase the dragon / the water will turn to cherry wine." The music game played with this dragon is not for sissies.

Sometimes, though, a dragon is just a dragon, and dragons need to be slain; it's their destiny, their reason for being—to die and give the world a hero. We slay personal dragons every day, and sometimes art is the sword.

"Then they talk like they know you / They don't know you."

We don't know who the trouble child is, kept in a sterilized room, with a wrong attitude. Or who the peacock is, afraid to parade. Does he/she still live, waiting to break again, like the waves at Malibu, against a soundtrack of mysterious electric piano phrases gently slipping underneath faraway trumpet calls, plaintive as seagulls' cries?

Despite being "under the thumb of the maid," I sense some measure of hope for this trouble child in the healing balm of the music. The soundtrack slides and drifts like a surfer who's lost the wave but survives to surf another day.

We need bards and troubadours to tell our stories, no matter where they may take us. Raised on robbery, off on a hejira, listening to the hissing of summer lawns, seeing hexagrams in the heavens. It doesn't matter who the trouble child is. The lady navigates this vale of tears with her voice and through her art expands the tale into the universal.

II. A FEW TROUBLE CHILDREN I KNEW: (NAMES WITHHELD AND SOME FACTS BLURRED OUT OF PRIVACY AND RESPECT)

There once was a jazz drummer, never quite as well-known as, say, Art Blakey or Max Roach or Shelley Manne or Kenny Clarke, but as good as any of them and respected by his colleagues. He performed variously with Thelonious Monk, Duke Ellington, Dave Brubeck, John Coltrane, Miles Davis, Charles Mingus, Art Pepper, et al. I remember a night at a friend's apartment in Los Angeles. The drummer, sitting in a rocking chair, extended a heavily bandaged hand. He was nursing an abscess caused by missing a vein in the back of his hand with a spike full of heroin. Later in the night, he asked for a ride home to Crenshaw. He got in the car, toting most of his clothes in a Hefty bag. A warm thank-you and goodbye, and he disappeared into a smoggy, smelly L.A. night. He died a few years later, all too soon.

I think often of a friend and fellow traveler; a brother in music and humor, a guitar player and composer of beautiful songs, messages from a vast, humane mind and soul. We went off with our mates to play music and maybe get famous. Along the way we met the dragon. I escaped with enough burns and claw marks to make me believe in the power of sheer will to survive. My friend was not so lucky. He chased the dragon into the future and, ultimately, succumbed to its ravages. Again, gone way too soon, leaving behind his children and his music. Rest easy, brother, your genes travel on. The list of the lost grows ever longer; I wrote this piece for them.

This is what "Trouble Child" means to me.

SHADOWS AND LIGHT

Every picture has its shadows
And it has some source of light
Blindness
Blindness and sight
The perils of benefactors
The blessings of parasites
Blindness
Blindness and sight
Threatened by all things
Devil of cruelty
Drawn to all things
Devil of delight
Mythical devil
Of the ever-present laws
Governing
Blindness
Blindness and sight

Suntans in reservation dining rooms
Pale miners in their lantern rays
Night
Night and day
Hostage smiles on presidents
Freedom scribbled in the subway
It's like night
Night and day
Threatened by all things
God of cruelty
Drawn to all things
God of delight
Mythical god of the everlasting laws
Governing
Day
Day and night

Critics of all expression
Judges in black and white
Saying it's wrong
Saying it's right
Compelled by prescribed standards
Or some ideals we fight
For wrong
Wrong and right
Threatened by all things
Man of cruelty—
Mark of Cain
Drawn to all things
Man of delight—
Born again
Born again
Man of the laws
The ever-broken laws
Governing
Wrong
Wrong and right
Governing
Wrong
Wrong and right
Wrong and right

LIGHT AND SHADOWS

PATRICIA SMITH

Shadows insist soft collison, turn every surface
to unwitnessed underbelly scarred and denied
in the moonwash. Suddenly, a splash of shine
illumes the chiming chaos, spotlights the gentle
atrocity of hours. Every picture brags a facet
that can't be swallowed, a shifting narrative,
muddled and indigo, that strains its borders.
In this version of this tale, every character
is composed of canine teeth, every character
croons night from a shuttered throat. Call him
horned. Call her a mistake of scarlet. Call them
bellowed verbs, incumbents, terrible infants.
The sky folds forward, sputters, erupts a kind of

light. Despite your brief and bright addiction
to cigarettes and myth, you believe unerringly
in the real. The sun had considered not rising.
Clawing for sight, the devil is forced to shift gears,
stuff his chafed and yellowed horns into the silk
innards of a nice hat. In our revised tale, at least
one character is steered toward a clichéd beauty,
beauty which separates eerily into black and white.
Black had considered not being wrong.
Brightness around its edges doesn't keep day from
saying ugly out loud. Born again simply means you
have at least twice resisted the sugar-coo of elegy.
Blindness governs everything we see and don't.

Shadows, with rearranged bruise, draw us to all
things, keep us giddily entertained while rumors
of revolution quiver our constitution. Our fists

are always cocked, which makes Sunday brunch
awkward. Instead, we read newspapers to one
another, we let exclamation settle on our skin,
we hand over the job of wrongness and rightness,
we succumb. It is impossible to look directly into
a shadow. We are crafted of impossible shadows.
Cain, what have you done? We are forced to admit
that a perfectly-angled shadow can make even
murder look necessary. Admit it now, that you rest
well here, would rather no one ever flips on the

light switch, bathing us in backslap, revealing our
two faces—black, white, right, wrong. The travesty
is that we must choose. The final version of this
story is pliable, blasted through with limelight,
capable of several surprise endings. Stand up tall,
straighten your skirt, slick down your hair, mind
that zipper. Put your best face, whichever it is,
forward. Ignore that insistent fanfare, the rollick
of drums in the country of your chest. You are where
we can all see you. Whether or not we choose to
look is a matter of contention. You have given
everything you are to the light. If you want to
increase your chances of being seen, sing. Sing.

I guess I'm an odd Joni fan. After all, I was a little colored girl growing up on the West Side of Chicago—the part of town everyone told you to stay away from—and the order of the day was R&B, gut-bucket blues, constant Motown and maybe a smattering of jazz.

But I was a bit of a the rebel, achingly curious about the "stories" in music, so I'd sneak a tinny little transistor into my bed at night, and that act of defiance opened up the world. When I first heard Joan Baez (I know, I know, that's not Joni, but I'm getting there)—staticky, "experimental," her voice bluewater clear—I knew I had sisters I'd never met. As I grew older, I hungrily gathered names, scoured stores for used records, wanted to learn more about this parallel world of light and lyric I wasn't privy to.

When I plopped the needle down on Joni's album *Blue*, I cried a little. Here were tales of smoke and sugar that went far beyond the "he/she done me wrong" I was accustomed to. As I listened to "A Case of You" over and over, I thought I'd tiptoed up to royalty. Later, I learned how many ways there were to fold her music into mine, to make her a part of my soundtrack, an essential thread in the fabric I wrapped around me.

Why "Light and Shadows"? Because inherent in her gorgeous lines, I heard the difference between who I was expected to be, and how music shined an insistent light on a life far, far beyond that. Joni won't quit. And neither will I.

COYOTE

No regrets Coyote
We just come from such different sets of circumstance
I'm up all night in the studios
And you're up early on your ranch
You'll be brushing out a brood mare's tail
While the sun is ascending
And I'll just be getting home with my reel to reel...
There's no comprehending
Just how close to the bone
And the skin
And the eyes
And the lips you can get
And still feel so alone
And still feel related
Like stations in some relay
You're not a hit and run driver
No, no
Racing away
You just picked up a hitcher
A prisoner of the white lines on the freeway

We saw a farmhouse burning down
In the middle of nowhere
In the middle of the night
And we rolled right past that tragedy
Till we turned into some road house lights
Where a local band was playing
Locals were up kicking and shaking on the floor
And the next thing I know
That Coyote's at my door
He pins me in a corner and he won't take "No!"
He drags me out on the dance floor
And we're dancing close and slow

Now, he's got a woman at home
He's got another woman down the hall
He seems to want me anyway!
Why'd you have to get so drunk
And lead me on that way
You just picked up a hitcher
A prisoner of the white lines on the freeway

I looked a Coyote right in the face
On the road to Baljennie near my old home town
He went running thru the whisker wheat
Chasing some prize down
And a hawk was playing with him
Coyote was jumping straight up and making passes
He had those same eyes
Just like yours
Under your dark glasses
Privately probing the public rooms
And peeking thru keyholes in numbered doors
Where the players lick their wounds
And take their temporary lovers
And their pills and powders
To get them thru this passion play
No regrets Coyote
I just get off up aways
You just picked up a hitcher
A prisoner of the white lines on the freeway

Coyote's in the coffee shop
He's staring a hole in his scrambled eggs
He picks up my scent on his fingers
While he's watching the waitresses' legs
He's too far from the Bay of Fundy
From appaloosas and eagles and tides
And the air conditioned cubicles
And the carbon ribbon rides
Are spelling it out so clear
Either he's going to have to stand and fight
Or take off out of here
I tried to run away myself
To run away and wrestle with my ego
And with this flame
You put here in this Eskimo
In this hitcher
In this prisoner
Of the fine white lines
Of the white lines on the free
Free
Way

COYOTE

TERESE KARMEL

Each evening I hear packs of coyotes making their journey across my yard to their daytime lairs—free spirits crying out to each other in the dark.

Years ago their "whoo-whoo-ing"—a cross between the hoot of an owl and the bark of a dog—frightened me enough to make sure our cat du jour was safely inside. But more recently, I have come to anticipate their music. On days they take a separate route, I fear for them, hopeful that their nighttime excursions have not ended at the rifle point of some hunter who hasn't learned to live and let live.

And so it is with those night creatures in mind that I settled on Joni Mitchell's slinky, evocative "Coyote" as my personal tribute to her, a song she herself chose to sing on the November 1976 album *The Last Waltz*, the final work of The Band. It is a fast-paced song with subtle instrumentation—almost like that of a jazz rhythm section—complemented by her frantic strumming.

"Coyote" is from the 1976 album *Hejira*, which means "flight" in Arabic. And indeed it is an album about flight and restlessness, enclosure and freedom. Mitchell wrote the songs while traveling across country by herself. She said of the work, it has a "restless feeling throughout it... the sweet loneliness of solitary travel."

The songs whiz by, like a traveler passing landmarks on a highway: "Amelia," about navigator Amelia Earhart, who was "swallowed by the sky" and like the singer "had a dream to fly"; "Blue Motel Room," in which the singer is traveling with "road maps / From two dozen states" but is torn by desire for the boy she left behind. This conflict between life on the road and the demands of professional commitment and a serious relationship (as in "Song for Sharon") runs through the album, but in "Coyote" she appears to reach a still point in her restless life. "Coyote" reflects this endless debate between comfort, familiarity and the desire to be free, a double-edged sword that drew me to Joni Mitchell decades ago.

Who among us has not been consumed by this dilemma? Who among us has chosen to hug the shore rather than cast out into deep waters, to walk away from the gaming table instead of rolling the dice and, as a result of decisions made years past, spent much of the rest of our lives wondering "what if?"

I have and I have not: a gambler by nature, I'm certainly not afraid to bet a long shot or draw to an inside straight. In many ways my life as a reporter has been unconventional, with its odd hours, its sometimes dangerous environments (among my beats were prisons and crime), its need to ask the loved one of someone who has just died, "how is it with you?" or as Joni Mitchell says in "Coyote," a life of taking "pills and powders" to get "thru this passion play." But there have been safe sides: marriage, though short-lived, kids, conventional hobbies like reading, opera, cooking, shopping—these havens have also defined my life.

Can you have it all? This is the question that haunts Joni Mitchell, but in "Coyote," she seems to opt for the life of the road, the life of one-night stands with a "coyote" of a man in a road house, a rural Canadian ranch hand—perhaps someone she might have ended up with had her life not taken a different turn—a traveler in the night who, has also left his comfort zone. The irony is that the freedom of the road is not freedom at all; in fact, she is a slave to her choice. She is up "all night in the studios" just as Coyote is up at dawn "brushing out a brood-mare's tail."

Their fleeting intimacy is graphically represented—"how close to the bone / And the skin / And the eyes / And the lips you can get"—yet is protection against true intimacy. Mitchell seems to come to terms with her life, repeating the phrase "no regrets" twice in the song. She is in touch with her choice as a "prisoner of the white lines on the freeway," the California highway far from her rural Canadian home. Each verse ends with the reminder that she is this prisoner but the last time she sings it, the charged word "free" is ironically repeated twice. It is haunting, to be sure, but it is said with confidence, not self-pity.

Among my professions is that of a literature instructor at a state college. Some anthologies give a (well deserved) nod to contemporary songwriters. For example, it's not unusual to find the lyrics of Dylan's "Blowin in the Wind" or McCartney and Lennon's "Michelle," or Jagger and Richards' "Ruby Tuesday" somewhere among the works of Keats, Tennyson and Frost. In fact, Dylan was among those mentioned as a possible winner of the 2010 Nobel Prize in Literature but that honor went to ninety-year-old Swedish poet Tomas Tranströmer, whose work was praised as a "progression from concrete reality to a heightened state of awareness."

Although any number of Mitchell's songs belongs in these pantheons of poets, I've never seen the lyrics of "River" or "Blue" or "Carey" or yes, "Coyote," in an anthology. And why not? This is a writer who uses the same tools as every great poet to create her songs: most likely plucked from her past, she draws from concrete experiences to weave abstract observations about love and death, isolation and community, freedom and oppression—in short, the marrow of life—so that the rest of us can better understand ourselves and the world around us. When I hear a Joni Mitchell song, I do, indeed, move from "concrete reality to a heightened state of awareness."

And so many nights as I fall asleep, my last thoughts are of Joni Mitchell as I think about those coyotes whose cries will be the last thing I hear—cries through which they reach out to each other—cries, hopefully, that don't lead to danger for them, so that they may continue to roam the free freeways where their lives take them.

FURRY SINGS THE BLUES

Old Beale Street is coming down
Sweeties' Snack Bar
Boarded up now
And Egles the Tailor and the Shine Boy's gone
Faded out with ragtime blues
Handy's cast in bronze
And he's standing in a little park
With his trumpet in his hand
Like he's listening back to the good old bands
And the click of high heeled shoes
Old Furry sings the blues
Propped up in his bed
With his dentures and his leg removed
And Ginny's there
For her kindness and Furry's beer
She's the old man's angel overseer

Pawn shops glitter like gold tooth caps
In the grey decay
They chew the last few dollars off old Beale Street's carcass
Carrion and mercy
Blue and silver sparkling drums
Cheap guitars, eye shades and guns
Aimed at the hot blood of being no one
Down and out in Memphis Tennessee
Old Furry sings the blues
You bring him smoke and drink and he'll play for you
It's mostly muttering now
And sideshow spiel
But there was one song he played
I could really feel...
"Old Furry's got nobody
Old Furry's got nobody"

There's a double bill murder at the New Daisy
The old girl's silent across the street
She's silent—
Waiting for the wrecker's beat
Silent—
Staring at her stolen name
Diamond boys and satin dolls
Bourbon laughter
Ghosts
History falls
To parking lots and shopping malls
As they tear down old Beale Street
Old Furry sings the blues
He points a bony finger at you and says
"I don't like you"
Everybody laughs as if it's the old man's standard joke
But it's true
We're only welcome for our drink and smoke

W. C. Handy I'm rich and I'm fey
And I'm not familiar with what you played
But I get such strong impressions of your heyday
Looking up and down old Beale Street
Ghosts of the darktown society
Come right out of the bricks at me
Like it's a Saturday night
They're in their finery
Dancing it up and making deals
Furry sings the blues
Why should I expect that old guy to give it to me true-blue
Fallen to hard luck
And time
And other thieves
While our limo is shining on his shanty street
Old Furry sings the blues

JONI, YOU'RE A RICH MAN, TOO

CORNELIUS EADY

"How Does It Feel To Be One Of The Beautiful People?"
John Lennon

"W.C. Handy, I'm rich and I'm fey"
Joni Mitchell

Sometimes, by the simple act of zigging left instead of zagging right, or turning my New-York-City-Always-Keep-Your-Eyes-Front towards the direction of some odd startle, I will stumble upon a weird life moment. If it's a lucky day, it'll be something more amusing than dangerous or depressing.

This afternoon, one hit as I was climbing the stairs towards my stationary bike at the gym in my neighborhood.

This gym's a bedazzling place; glass, steel, wood, big screen TVs, cool music, cute coffee bar, which I use on the afternoons I don't take a walk.

It's truly Coolsville, but some days, it's an effort to go in. The problem is simply this: Almost everyone at the gym is young and beautiful, and I am... not.

This isn't a topic for pity or debate; I'm not ugly (not at least—thank the Gods—to my wife) but I know I have entered the land of the buff and toned, the wheatgrass fed, the accessory dancers.

They are working at maintaining a certain body image. They have a routine, a trainer, a lingo, while I'm just trying to stay a little less lumpy. We both know the difference. Do I belong there? I feel lucky I'm not asked for anything more than a membership card when I walk in.

Just let me bike in peace is all my body asks, as I swing through the door, blinders on, iTunes blasting, up to the front desk. Card in, grab water, buy water, check coat (in winter) and peel towards the stairs.

These are the stairs I am climbing when the Beatles' "Baby, You're A Rich Man" rocks through my headphones.

Here's that weird moment: climbing up the stairs towards the large, well-lit, media buzzed room with those lyrics in my ears, I suddenly realized they all might think me a bit of an odd duck here; I may not be the Jet Set Lennon is probably referring to/half-mocking in his song. But am I poor? No. No longer. And poetry delivered me here.

"How does it feel?" Lennon, the dead, rich, working class hero sings.

How should I feel?

Joni Mitchell's great "blues" about the blues takes place right in the middle of that ambivalence. She's taken on the topic before, in her great song "For Free" from her album *Ladies Of The Canyon*, but this time, instead of a nameless, faceless street musician, who she listens to from a distance, after a day spent "shopping for jewels," we find ourselves sitting in a room on Beale Street in Memphis, Tennessee, with a real blues man, Furry Lewis, who was a contemporary of and played with W.C. Handy.

What are the blues, if not consequences, sung? I think one of the reasons the greatest of the singer-songwriters of the late '60s and '70s are poets is that their lyrics take on the duty of the poem as they dig beneath the surface of things unspoken— love, sex, marriage, money, race—and in Joni Mitchell's song about Furry Lewis, she leads us to consider the wrecked 1970s streets the music springs from; the blues man, beloved but somewhat objectified by his white fans; urban renewal; fickle luck; how the lines of American history, poverty and mythologies co-mingle and blur.

The greatness of "Furry Sings The Blues" has always been that Joni Mitchell resists the urge to resolve anything in the song; she simply and honestly lets all the elements, all the truths and contradictions hang in the air ("Carrion and mercy," as she puts it) and sings a faithful portrait of a diminished man, stuck in a diminished city as the gears of his life spin, toothless.

In "Furry Sings The Blues," the blues isn't a bunch of notes; it's the way fate bends a life; his, and hers. Her good luck—the blessings of peace and options (the "shining" limo that brought her there will take her back to the life her music has given her)—and his hard luck co-exist in the same small universe of a room.

Joni Mitchell somehow wrestles with, translates, then sings the tension and miscommunication in that room as Furry sings, the rage he spurts at his visitors (who, after all, just came to seek out his younger, long-gone self), the complications that arise when one goes looking for a song, and instead finds a city and a man, soaked in disappointments. She never decides if she's one of the angels or thieves in the room, but then if she did, we'd never get so powerful a song.

HEJIRA

I'm traveling in some vehicle
I'm sitting in some café
A defector from the petty wars that shell-shock love away
There's comfort in melancholy
When there's no need to explain
It's just as natural as the weather in this moody sky today
In our possessive coupling
So much could not be expressed
So now I am returning to myself
These things that you and I suppressed
I see something of myself in everyone
Just at this moment of the world
As snow gathers like bolts of lace
Waltzing on a bridal girl

You know it never has been easy
Whether you do or you do not resign
Whether you travel the breadth of extremities
Or stick to some straighter line
Now here's a man and a woman sitting on a rock
They're either going to thaw out or freeze
Listen...
Strains of Benny Goodman coming through the snow and the pinewood trees
I'm porous with travel fever
But you know I'm so glad to be on my own
Still somehow the slightest touch of a stranger
Sets up a trembling in my bones
I know
No one's going to show me everything
We all come and go unknown
Each so deep and so superficial
Between the forceps and the stone

Well I looked at the granite markers
Those tributes to finality—to eternity
And then I looked at myself here
Chicken scratching for my immortality
In the church they light the candles
And the wax rolls down like tears
There is the hope and the hopelessness
I've witnessed all these years
We're only particles of change
I know
I know
Orbiting around the sun
But how can I have that lofty point of view
When I'm bound and tied to someone
White flags of winter chimneys
Waving—truce
Against the moon
In the mirrors of a modern bank
From the window of my hotel room

I'm traveling in some vehicle
I'm sitting in some café
A defector from the petty wars
Until
Love sucks me back that way

HEJIRA—SO MUCH COULD NOT BE EXPRESSED

BESSY REYNA

I have often wondered how someone who lives thousands of miles away from where I grew up, who doesn't know me, who doesn't even know that I exist, can describe images, colors and feelings as if they had been pulled from my own life. But, from the very first time I heard Joni Mitchell's songs, that was exactly how I felt. Time and time again she has encouraged me to look at myself, my past; the roads taken and avoided. It is because of this unique communion with her that I have carried copies of her songs with me regardless of where I lived. Somewhere in my room there has always been a private Joni collection—from LPs to cassettes, to CDs—kept together, and always within reach, so her words could soothe me or shake me, but always make me feel alive.

Journeys seem to be part of her life and mine. Physical or spiritual searches for something, without quite knowing exactly what it is we need to find. Joni extends her hands out to me and invites me to follow her in unknown personal adventures or recollections.

"I'm sitting in some café"

Listening to "Hejira" I am transported back to the times when I sat in some café with a friend I was not supposed to be in love with. We drank espresso, admiring sunsets over the Pacific Ocean in Panama City. With each refill, I tried to touch her fingers in an intentional—but seemingly casual—touch as I handed her the packets of sugar I knew she would empty, and then twist and discard, just like she was going to do with me. My first of many "petty wars" with no winners, just bodies left on the battlefield.

"Now here's a man and a woman sitting on a rock"

The man and the woman sitting on a rock are free to kiss each other, embrace and show their love in public. We couldn't. We had to hide everything, always pretending not to desire and not to love the person whose body was a mirror image. Those feelings were hidden for so long that they became like smudged carbon copies of who we were.

"...I am returning to myself / These things that you and I suppressed"

"Hejira" makes me want to put my memories in a shredder and pick up the strips at random. Each line contains a fragment of what I once called love, or attraction, or rejection, or betrayal.

"In the church they light the candles"

Churches are for people who believe in something I can't understand. If I go inside a church, it is for a funeral service, or to admire the artwork, the history. But, while visiting the Hagia Sophia in Thessaloniki, surrounded by icons, I was overtaken by the reverence of the place. I lit a candle in memory of a very special friend and mentor who had died years before. At the church there was a small table, with a basket overflowing with pieces of paper displaying names of loved ones who were to be remembered with a prayer and a candle. I felt an overwhelming urge to drop some money in the box and to write my friend's name, in Greek letters, to make sure that the god who guarded the church would take my message to her.

I thought I would travel far enough to be on my own: from Panama to Massachusetts, only to learn that what I wanted to forget or run away from was not controlled by physical distance.

The exceptional beauty of Joni Mitchell's words is that she makes me think of my past while, at the same time, describing someone else's present. She is a link to our common humanity.

I imagine that I'm now at a safe distance from the past, but then again, "love can suck me back" at any moment. It's happened before. I can only hope that when it does I might be sitting in some café, enjoying the feeling of the "trembling in my bones" without having to hide it.

SONG FOR SHARON

I went to Staten Island, Sharon
To buy myself a mandolin
And I saw the long white dress of love
On a storefront mannequin
Big boat chuggin' back with a belly full of cars
All for something lacy
Some girl's going to see that dress
And crave that day like crazy

Little Indian kids on a bridge up in Canada
They can balance and they can climb
Like their fathers before them
They'll walk the girders of the Manhattan skyline
Shine your light on me Miss Liberty
Because as soon as this ferry boat docks
I'm headed to the church
To play Bingo
Fleece me with the gamblers' flocks

I can keep my cool at poker
But I'm a fool when love's at stake
Because I can't conceal emotion
What I'm feeling's always written on my face
There's a gypsy down on Bleecker Street
I went in to see her as a kind of joke
And she lit a candle for my love luck
And eighteen bucks went up in smoke

Sharon, I left my man
At a North Dakota junction
And I came out to the "Big Apple" here
To face the dream's malfunction

Love's a repetitious danger
You'd think I'd be accustomed to
Well I do
Accept the changes
At least
Better than I used to do

A woman I knew just drowned herself
The well was deep and muddy
She was just shaking off futility
Or punishing somebody
Friends—calling up all day yesterday
All emotions and abstractions
It seems we all live so close to that line
And so far from satisfaction

Dora says "Have children"
Mama and Betsy say "Find yourself a charity
Help the needy and the crippled
Or put some time into Ecology"
Well, there's a wide wide world of noble causes
And lovely landscapes to discover
But all I really want to do right now
Is... find another lover!

When we were kids in Maidstone, Sharon
I went to every wedding in that little town
To see the tears and the kisses
And the pretty lady in the white lace wedding gown
And walking home on the railroad tracks
Or swinging on the playground swing
Love stimulated my illusions
More than anything

And when I went skating after Golden Reggie
You know it was white lace I was chasing
Chasing dreams
Mama's nylons
Underneath my cowgirl jeans
He showed me first you get the kisses
And then you get the tears
But the ceremony of the bells and lace
Still veils this reckless fool here

Now there are twenty-nine skaters on Wollman Rink
Circling in singles and in pairs
In this vigorous anonymity
A blank face at the window
Stares
And stares
And stares and stares
And the power of reason
And the flowers of deep feeling
Seem to serve me
Only to deceive me

Sharon you've got a husband
And a family and a farm
I've got the apple of temptation
And a diamond snake around my arm
But you still have your music
And I've still got my eyes on the land and the sky
You sing for your friends and your family
I'll walk green pastures by and by

JONI

SHARON BELL VEER

Until my sister phoned to tell me that she had just bought Joni's latest album, *Hejira*, and that there was a song on the album written for me called "Song for Sharon," I knew nothing about it. I was excited, but honestly, I was also mystified. When *Hejira* was released, I had not seen Joni for some time, and I wondered, "Why me?"; but listening to the song and reading the words took me on a journey—back to Maidstone, back to when we were little kids in that little town, back to holidays at the Anderson homes in both North Battleford and Saskatoon, back to a road trip with Joni and her parents through the states and parts of Canada, back to the first time I reconnected with her after fame found her, and finally forward to my personal understanding of why she wrote this poem and what our friendship really means to me today.

I must admit that when I first heard "Song for Sharon," I felt some sadness as I listened to the last stanza. It seemed to me that Joni was searching for something solid and ordinary, something that perhaps she desired, if only briefly. I wondered if there was some longing for the life that I have, but that her passionate and creative urges would only allow her to glimpse in passing. The song painted a vivid picture of the place I believed Joni to be in her life at that time; the haunting quality of the music pulled me into the song in which she was deeply connected with her roots, or so it seemed to me.

The song conjured up all kinds of images and memories for me as well. "Walking on the railroad tracks" was a favorite pastime of ours, and on our road trip I remember walking on tracks and Joni being afraid that we might encounter snakes, because we'd found a dead one earlier (she was quite terrified of snakes as I remember, and I had no fear of them). That summer of 1958, Pat Boone's "April Love" was the big hit and our young teenaged hearts would beat a little faster every time we heard it. Even then, "love stimulated my illusions more than anything" was true. Joni always was, and still is, fun-loving, but her artistic side was also present back then—present in the tree she painted on her bedroom wall, and present in the moods that sometimes caused her to withdraw a little into herself.

I admire Joni's creative genius more than I can say, but as importantly, I admire her creative integrity—integrity I saw when my husband and I visited her during her first concert in Saskatoon so many years ago. I sensed then that she would always be true to her spirit and follow the path she knew was right for her. Her desire to embrace new challenges, as is evidenced by her work with the Alberta Ballet's "The Fiddle and the Drum"—stunning in its message and beauty—and her commitment to editing the film version of the production underscore both her work ethic and her desire to continually grow.

Over the years there have been only a few occasions when I have been able to spend some time with Joni, but the amazing thing is that, in spite of these brief encounters, I have always felt a connection—the kind of connection that allows us to pick up where we left off the last time we were together and share stories from our childhood, as well as what is going on in our lives all these years later. I have not been a part of her life as a continually evolving artist; she has friends—many famous—who belong there. Rather I belong in the category of "do you remember the time…?" and we share a laugh in the retelling of an old story. Her "I love you" as we left her mother's graveside service—our final goodbye to an amazing woman—and my "I love you too," as we went our separate ways, is a reminder to me that we share a bond that will stand the test of time and distance. She has a piece of my heart, and I hope that I have a piece of hers.

SISTOWBELL LANE

Sisotowbell Lane...
Noah is fixing the pump in the rain
He brings us no shame
We always knew that he always knew
Up over the hill...
Jovial neighbors come down when they will
With stories to tell
Sometimes they do
Yes sometimes we do
We have a rocking chair
Each of us rocks his share
Eating muffin buns and berries
By the steamy kitchen window
Sometimes we do
Our tongues turn blue

Sisotowbell Lane
Anywhere else now would seem very strange
The seasons are changing
Every day
In every way
Sometimes it is spring
Sometimes it is not anything
A poet can sing
Sometimes we try
Yes we always try
We have a rocking chair
Some days we rock and stare
At the woodlands and the grasslands
And the badlands 'cross the river...
Sometimes we do
We like the view

Sisotowbell Lane

Go to the city—you'll come back again

To wade thru the grain

You always do

Yes we always do

Come back to the stars

Sweet well water and pickling jars

We'll lend you the car

We always do

Yes sometimes we do

We have a rocking chair

Someone is always there

Rocking rhythms

While they're waiting

With the candle in the window...

Sometimes we do...

We wait for you

THE CANDLE IN THE WINDOW

SUE/SIOUX TABBAT WURZEL

Stumbling through the dark forest of adolescence, I knew enough to recognize magic when I came upon it. I first saw Joni on a tiny platform stage with a gritty brick wall behind her. I had taken a train from my suburban home in Westchester into Manhattan, then I'd walked from Grand Central to Penn Station in the chilly dusk, finally taking a train to Philadelphia. I had come to see who Joni was. For once I was grateful for having liberal, laissez-faire parents who had never given me a curfew or questioned my whereabouts.

I was looking for Joni because I had seen her name as the person credited for having written "Urge for Going." That was all I knew. She had no album. In the pre-internet world of the mid-'60s, I had the fun of playing detective to hunt her down. Having ardently loved the movie *The World of Henry Orient*, in which two teenage girls follow an adored adult pianist through the streets of Manhattan, I had some ideas about how to go about my mission. And this was the night when I was finally blasting off. I may have been shy, but I was also spunky. I had found a tiny ad in the paper informing me that Joni would be playing at a club called The Second Fret.

When I saw her, it took my breath away. When she began to sing, I was transported, transfixed, enchanted. I fell in love, in a pure and platonic way. I felt like I was witnessing a miracle, because I was. In some ineffable way, her words, her haunting melodies, her elusive guitar playing made me feel known, understood. My feelings were a tribute to the universality of brilliant art emanating from the "heart and mind" of one person and flowing directly into the "heart and mind" of another. My feelings were a tribute to Joni's gift.

After she finished her set, she stepped off the stage and disappeared behind a doorway. She smiled at me as she passed by.

The next night I made the trek back, having somehow managed to sit at a school desk in the interim. As Joni made her way through the small crowd towards the door, she paused and said to me, "You'll get bored if you come every night."

"I won't get bored," I protested. My eyes welled up. I didn't want to be banished from this kingdom.

On the third night, Joni took my hand. "If you're going to keep coming," she said, "you can keep me company between sets." That was the beginning. That night I returned to my family's home, a place where the dinner table conversation always tended towards erudite critiques of Italian opera and other such matters, which were foreign to my adolescent heart. I wrote a poem in my diary before I went to sleep.

> *Internal rhymes are Joni's kind*
> *"They're fool's gold" scolds the Tabbat test*
> *I'm mining now in my own mind*
> *I'm Sioux and know what Sioux loves best*

Many years later, Joni's friend Jane told me that, when I had first appeared upon the scene, Joni had told her with incredulity,

"I think I might have a fan!"

I was mute in Joni's presence for many years. I followed her from club to club, and later from college campus to college campus. Then came the charmed night I followed her to the miracle of Carnegie Hall, the very place where the girls in Henry Orient had seen their beloved pianist perform. Joni was unfailingly kind, in spite of my inability to express myself, to speak. And, as much as I had wished for the whole world to celebrate her as I did, her rise to fame was difficult for me, in my awkward hesitancy and self-doubt. Even my classmates wanted a piece of Joni now, as if she were some sort of commodity, rather than the person I so adored. Jane took me under her wing and gave me lessons in "existential edge." She told me that all people are equal, that I was Joni's equal. I didn't believe her then. Now, having passed the milestone of my sixtieth birthday, I have long since found my voice, and developed a deep and abiding adult friendship with Joni (to the extent that either of us is a bona fide grown-up). I now know that Jane was right—all people are equal—but I still don't believe her. I am not Joni's equal. I am not a creative genius.

One of the songs that captivated me then, and that now dwells within me as part of my own personal mythology, is "Sisotowbell Lane," in which Joni innocently and without guile refers to herself as "a poet" who "can sing." With few words, this poem portrays a world as cozy, safe and self-contained as if it were inside a snow globe. For me, it conjures a yearning for a childhood different from the one I had, while, at the same time, creating within me the feeling that I can—even now—be held, protected and rocked. In this safe haven, there is "no shame." This song lulls me. It soothes me. I like to picture myself "Eating muffin buns and berries / By the steamy kitchen window."

Setting aside the beautiful, rhythmic, mesmerizing music, this poem's enchantment lies in its economical and lovely imagery, its structure, and in the universality of the comfort it offers. Every time I read or listen to "Sisotowbell Lane," I am astonished anew at the perfection of Joni's choice of words. I marvel at the word "wade," a verb usually reserved for water, as I picture returning to the land "to wade through the grain." And who wouldn't want to come home at night to loved ones who are "Rocking rhythms / While they're waiting / With the candle in the window"? I know I would. As young as Joni was when she wrote this piece, she knew to give each stanza a perfect structure. Each verse is filled with brief, painterly descriptions, laying a full palette before the mind's eye. Joni knew intuitively to end each stanza with the inclusive, communal, first person plural—"Our tongues turn blue," and "We like the view," and "We wait for you." The "we" is all-encompassing and makes the poem feel like an open invitation to come home.

On another note, this poem is sadly all too pertinent today, as we humans continue to ravage the natural beauty of our planet. The protective glass of my imagined snow globe has remained durable in my mind, but the real world's shielding ozone layer has been fractured. Noah, a good man, and one who survived the floods of Biblical times, "is fixing the pump in the rain." Few people were talking about climate change or rising seas when Joni wrote that line. She had an overview, an awareness and a premonition. When, in "Woodstock," she said, "We've got to get ourselves back to the garden," she meant it. We all need to treasure "the woodlands and the grasslands" and the "sweet well water" that still remain. I once heard Joni say that nature was her religion.

"Sisotowbell" is an acronym, created by Joni. It stands for "Somehow, in spite of trouble, ours will be ever lasting love." In the safe bubble of the self-contained universe depicted in the poem, love will always transcend conflict. Families will remain intact. Friendships will endure. The candle in the window will always light the way back home.

BLACK CROW

There's a crow flying
Black and ragged
Tree to tree
He's black as the highway that's leading me
Now he's diving down
To pick up on something shiny
I feel like that black crow
Flying
In a blue sky

I took a ferry to the highway
Then I drove to a pontoon plane
I took a plane to a taxi
And a taxi to a train
I've been traveling so long
How'm I ever going to know my home
When I see it again
I'm like a black crow
Flying
In a blue, blue sky

In search of love and music
My whole life has been
Illumination
Corruption
And diving
Diving
Diving
Diving
Diving down to pick up on every shiny little thing
Just like that black crow
Flying
In a blue sky

I looked at the morning
After being up all night
I looked at my haggard face in the bathroom light
I looked out the window
And I saw that ragged soul take flight
I saw a black crow flying
In a blue sky
Oh I'm like a black crow
Flying
In a blue sky

BLACK CROW, BARE TREE

PIT PINEGAR

Sometimes a poet wonders *at*—
and sometimes *about*—his remark-
able attention to linguistic detail.
There's nothing lackadaisical
about the word *lackadaisical*,

for instance, nothing ambiguous
about the selection of *ambiguity*.
Why does it matter so much
that a crow's wings *slap* the air,
that the correct word conveys

sound as well as motion, as well as
an intimation of anger,
that the word have an *a* sound
that is somewhere between short
and long—the *a* of *gasp*, *clasp*,

snap, *fast*, *sand*, not the *a* in *ache*
and *able* or *ah* and *aha*, because
a crow (Should it be a raven?)
is landing on one of the larger
branches (not limbs) of an apple tree,

and all those *as* strung together
create a sound just right for
a large black bird alighting
in an apple tree long after
the apples have been harvested

(not picked) and the leaves
have fallen (not dropped).
Most of the time, a poet scours
the word-world for words that together
form an image that might lodge

in a reader's mind—*the world
is too much with us... in the room
the women come and go...
once upon a midnight dreary...
when I have fears that I may*

cease to be—but a poet knows
that not a single soul may read
his words; so why get wrapped up
in such precision? Is it about
creating order in the small world

of a poem? Or finding a home
in which to dwell wholly, if only
for a short while? Is it an act
of defiance, of will to create a world
that makes sense of all that might

otherwise remain senseless? Still,
once in awhile it must occur to a poet
that she—*and* the world—might be
better be served by the *yawk*
and strut of an actual crow,

by an actual apple plucked ripe
from an actual tree, turned into
cobbler or pie or served up
thinly sliced with cheese to assuage
simpler hungers, more easily satisfied.

I love crows—the size and shape of them, the sound of them, the strutting arrogance of them, the way they flock, sometimes by the thousands. When I was a kid, my cousins had a pet crow. He'd swoop through the house, steal shiny things and hide them in his hidey-hole in the rafters of the garage.

I love crow art—paintings, etchings, life-like sculptures of all sizes. I visit the Morrison Gallery in Kent, Connecticut, regularly, not just to view the current exhibit, but to commune with Peter Woytuk's larger- (or smaller-) than-life crows.

I love Joni Mitchell's song, "Black Crow." She likens herself to the black-as-highway crow diving down to pick up every shiny thing—the search for music and love. The long talks about the journey in search of all that's bright and shiny; and the implied dilemma: if we're eternally in flight, how will we recognize home when we come upon it?

Crows winter in my part of the world—central Connecticut. Some late afternoons, when the sun is low in the west, the sky in Hartford is black with crows looking for trees in which to roost for the night. They strut by the thousands in the open fields of the University of St. Joseph over the line in West Hartford.

One afternoon in this winter-of-abundant-snow, in the midst of a blizzard when the other birds folded themselves under the curled leaves of the rhododendrons or between the layers of a pine, a small flock of crows—perhaps ten—landed in my back yard.

It was a perfect snow day: Buddha's Delight tea steeping in a white porcelain teapot, Joni on the boom box, a modest gathering of crows visible through the slanting snow. Best of all, school out, I had nothing more pressing than to let my senses put it all together and to see what might come from the delicious combination of art and artifice, and the black and white of the natural world. In my experience, awareness combined with any confluence of events or images gives birth to something new, especially when beauty is involved; it seems to create an impulse to replicate what is beautiful in some way, not a replication of the thing itself, but the quality of beauty in whatever way we might be able to create it.

At the time of this particular confluence of beautiful things, I was working on a short story about loss, grief and failure to recover. I'd sent my character off to the island of Skiathos, in Greece, to see if a change of context could mitigate the all-consuming quality of her loss. There was a wind-twisted pine growing out of a rock at water's edge (in fact there is such a tree in that place); later that day, at my computer, a crow—related directly to ones from my back yard and Joni's—alighted in that tree in my story. Eventually, a draft or two later, I was forced to sacrifice the crow, artistically speaking; I needed a bird that would sit still for longer periods of time than do crows, one that might swoop down to nab a lizard after a lengthy vigil.

But the crow that couldn't do the work I needed it to do in that story didn't lift off and disappear. It became a presence in my creative consciousness. It became a symbol of awareness and observation. Weeks later, it became exactly the right bird to put into a poem about precision of language in poetry, the complexities of purpose and choice, a meditation about why poets—other writers, too, but especially poets—are so exacting in their use of language. I found myself holding Joni's crow and metaphor in my mind during the whole process, from snow day to story, to the space in between, to poem—the dives we make for what shines, for what attracts us during the journey: the pursuit of art, of home, our receptiveness to the generosities of awareness. I also tried to hold the question that she doesn't articulate precisely, but is certainly implicit in "Black

Crow": must we make a choice? By traveling (an artistic road), do we give up the possibility of home, in a conventional sense? And if it's true that we do, is it possible to re-define home so that we are not chronically bereft or in conflict?

It is significant that this winter, and during that particular blizzard of the crows, I had had to abandon my own definition of home and was bereft.

As any artist knows, the minute we let go of a song, a poem, a story, a painting, our creative intention becomes obscured by what the person who experiences the art brings to it. While he might bring his full awareness, he also brings who and what he is in that moment.

Grief-stricken on that psychically homeless day, I allowed myself to become fully aware of the almost limitless beauty of the storm, the crows, the music, the delicate, almost lilac-scented tea, the white-on-white of the pot. It was a choice to be aware of all that beauty. It was a choice to hold it simultaneously with homelessness and grief. It was a choice, much later, to see if I could write a poem about the choices involved in writing a poem... and it was a choice to consider the possibility that a home, however nomadic and solitary, might be found in creative process.

Joni's "Black Crow" accompanied me, start to finish, on the journey between that winter afternoon, a fiction on an island in Greece and, finally, a poem. A black crow, the highway, the metaphors, the questions raised by Joni's song, a meditation on definitions of home—all have been both companions and (pre)occupations. Inspiration is magical, intangible and, perhaps, never-ending. "Black Crow, Bare Tree" doesn't settle anything; it isn't an end point; it's simply a place to pause in a continuing meditation.

DREAMLAND

It's a long, long way from Canada
A long way from snow chains
Donkey vendors slicing coconut
No parkas to their name
Black babies covered in baking flour
The cook's got a carnival song
We're going to lay down someplace shady
With dreamland coming on
Dreamland, dreamland
Dreamland, dreamland

Walter Raleigh and Chris Columbus
Come marching out of the waves
And claim the beach and all concessions
In the name of the suntan slaves
I wrapped that flag around me
Like a Dorothy Lamour sarong
And I lay down thinking national
With dreamland coming on
Dreamland, dreamland
Dreamland, dreamland

Goodtime Mary and a fortune hunter
All dressed up to follow the drums
Mary in a feather hula-hoop
Miss Fortune with a rose on her big game gun
All saints, all sinners shining
Heed those trumpets all night long
Propped up on a samba beat
With dreamland coming on
Dreamland, dreamland
Dreamland, dreamland

Tar baby and the Great White Wonder
Talking over a glass of rum
Burning on the inside
With the knowledge of things to come
There's gambling out on the terrace
And midnight ramblin' on the lawn
As they lean toward temptation
With dreamland coming on
Dreamland, dreamland
Dreamland, dreamland

In a plane flying back to winter
In shoes full of tropic sand
A lady in a foreign flag
On the arm of her Marlboro Man
The hawk howls in New York City
Six foot drifts on Myrtle's lawn
As they push the recline buttons down
With dreamland coming on
Dreamland, dreamland
Dreamland, dreamland

African sand on the trade winds
And the sun on the Amazon
As they push the recline buttons down
With dreamland coming on
Dreamland, dreamland
Dreamland, dreamland

DREAMLAND

BARBARA LaFLESH

I dreamed I took a cruise
across that final river,
in a ferry lush with tourists.
Couples in evening clothes crowded the cash bar,
music pushed them to the dance floor.

I was young again, and beautiful enough
to lean against the ship's rail
and smoke a cigarette with casual disregard.
I disembarked in thick silky darkness
and met you there in the land of the dead.

We embraced as the shadows shifted
in the fire's glow. I tried to sip my drink
while you whispered into my neck.
While you conjured that helpless moan
in an old woman's dream.

I told you we had gathered after your death
to mourn the poems you'd never write,
your friends accustomed to your casual goodbye.
Trees waved shadows under the sluggish sun,
malt and tobacco sufficient incense.

In my dream I boarded the return ferry giddy,
flushed as the boatswain offered me his sideways stare.
The DJ off duty, a few passengers lingered on the deck,
the bartender dried the last glass.
The moonlight fell through the chilly dark.

The whispers rush by in a moment of wisdom
that comes before sleep.
Do you ever dream about your own elusive verse,
words moving together in a well-rehearsed dance,
the letters bending in to each other?

The extraordinary music, poetic lyrics and distinctive artwork of Joni Mitchell have become an essential influence on our culture. We hear a song and we are transported in an instant to another self in another time. Welcome to the land of dreams. A place we can visit in sleep or in escape. The land of desires, of spirits, of imagination propelled by genius and beauty. Daydreams, fantasy, astral dimensions. The alternate reality to our concrete selves. Dreams that spirit us away or move us toward a vision.

We have listened to the songs of Joni Mitchell in ecstasy and in grief, in love and in anger. We have cherished her voice and her style. We have lived with her songs flowing through our collective dreamland. They have accompanied our many days.

THE SILKY VEILS OF ARDOR

I am a poor wayfaring stranger
Traveling through all these highs and lows
I heard there was no sickness
No toil or danger
Just mercy and plenty
Where peaceful waters flow
Where peaceful waters flow

Come all you fair and tender school girls
Be careful now when you court young men
They are like the stars
On a summer morning
They sparkle up the night
And they're gone again
Daybreak—gone again

If I'd only seen
Through the silky veils of ardor
What a killing crime
This love can be
I would have locked up my heart
In a golden sheath of armor
And kept its crazy beating
Under strictest secrecy
High security

I wish I had the wings
Of Noah's pretty little white dove
So I could fly this raging river
To reach the one I love
But I have no wings
And the water is so wide
We'll have to row a little harder
It's just in dreams we fly
In my dreams we fly!

FOR JONI

AMY BYINGTON

Like my mother, I started having very strong intuitions and visions at around age thirty-five, mostly about family and close friends. I've continued to have these throughout my life, and most recently, at age seventy-eight, I had a particularly beautiful one about Joni Mitchell.

I saw Joni standing in a room with French doors flung open to the sky. She was standing in front of an open grand piano, which was in the back left corner of the room.

Two doves were flying out from the piano opening. Several doves were flying from Joni's uplifted arms.

I saw all of the doves flying across the room and out through the French doors, into the blue sky.

Different possibilities have crossed my mind regarding what this might mean.

I learned shortly after having this experience that Joni's Dad had passed on.

I am wondering if releasing the doves might have been an image of Joni sending peace to her Dad.

Or was it possibly connected to "Noah's pretty little white dove," in her gorgeous poem "The Silky Veils of Ardor"? This piece was unfamiliar to me until after the vision.

It doesn't matter.

What a magnificent vision it was.

GOD MUST BE A BOOGIE MAN

He is three
One's in the middle unmoved
Waiting
To show what he sees to the other two
To the one attacking—so afraid
And the one that keeps trying to love and trust
And getting himself betrayed
In the plan—
The divine plan
God must be a boogie man!

One's so sweet
So overly loving and gentle
He lets people in to his innermost sacred temple
Blind faith to care
Blind rage to kill
Why'd he let them talk him down
To cheap work and cheap thrills
In the plan—
The insulting plan
God must be a boogie man!

Which would it be
Mingus one or two or three
Which one do you think he'd want the world to see
Well, world opinion's not a lot of help
When a man's only trying to find out
How to feel about himself!
In the plan—
The cock-eyed plan
God must be a boogie man!

THE PLAN IS IN THE DOORWAY
FOR JONI MITCHELL AND IN MEMORY OF CHARLES MINGUS

FRED WAH

God could be a boogie man
But he's really Mr. In-Between
Part of a little notion
To stand in the doorway
Not wanting to be seen
Minding the commotion
But getting in the way

In 1963
You were coming thru the door
On West 37th
Hanging out with Mr. Howl
Digging the poetry scene
And starting to mess around
With Mr. In-Between

Riffing on the prairies plan
That post-War plan
To jump
Not caught up in the middle
But moving side-to-side

Real book or fake book
Sniffing out the charts ahead
How to find the door
And stand there in the way

Be three!
Affirmative!

Word's out
What we need to do
Is mess around
With Mr. In-Between

I was a music student and young poet in Vancouver in 1963 when a local, young folk singer, Joni Mitchell, showed up at a party with a crowd of poets and artists to meet Allen Ginsberg. Years later, though I always liked her singular music stylings, I was very impressed about her work with Charlie Mingus, a jazz hero of mine. I love the warmth of their collaboration.

THE WOLF THAT LIVES IN LINDSEY

Of the darkness in men's minds
What can you say
That wasn't marked by history
Or the TV news today
He gets away with murder
The blizzards come and go
The stab and glare and buckshot
Of the heavy heavy snow
It comes and goes
It comes and goes

His grandpa loved an empire
His sister loved a thief
And Lindsey loved the ways of darkness
Beyond belief
Girls in chilly blouses
The blizzards come and go
The stab and glare and buckshot
Of the heavy heavy snow
It comes and goes
It comes and goes

The cops don't seem to care
For derelicts or ladies of the night
They're weeds for yanking out of sight
If you're smart or rich or lucky
Maybe you'll beat the laws of man
But the inner laws of spirit
And the outer laws of nature
No man can
No
No man can

There lives a wolf in Lindsey
That raids and runs
Through the hills of Hollywood
And the downtown slums
He gets away with murder
The blizzards come and go
The stab and glare and buckshot
Of the heavy heavy snow
It comes and goes
It comes and goes
It comes and goes

ON "THE WOLF THAT LIVES IN LINDSEY"

PAUL LISICKY

There must be satisfaction in tuning down the bottom string of your guitar to C. Not just to play it, but to attack so that what comes out isn't a C at all but a blur of three notes. It buzzes and snaps. It splashes and keens. It is the sound of chaos, but it isn't the imitation chaos of those self-impressed electric guitar solos. It is something new. Joni makes her chaos on an acoustic guitar, and maybe she knows it's more unsettling to hear it like that. The instrument of the ballad, the instrument of tenderness, built of wood, built like a body. Curious to speak of its neck and its body, as if it were human, female, shaped around a sound hole. Not impermeable, not man-made, but avid and imperfect, capable of trembling with shock. Just like the tree that it comes from, hit by lightning on a summer night. And does that have something to do with why she's hitting the neck so hard? Well, only the singer knows.

> Girls in chilly blouses
> The blizzards come and go
> The stab and glare and buckshot
> Of the heavy heavy snow
> It comes and goes
> It comes and goes

Maybe she knows that even her dearest fans are going to pass over this song. No one's going to hear it. A song of murder, a song of murdering women, written and sung by a woman. Not righteous in its tone, but cool, seductive, lush. Certainly it must be hard to move through that sequence of chords without sweetening or tidying or embedding some message inside. Certainly it must make her a little sick. Excited too, but she can't deny the sickness. By God, she's had enough. Too many songs conjuring up a persona that can't always be in sync with herself. That persona! Quick to laugh, quick to show off her large and beautiful mouth, quick to let her gaze fall. Shy, seductive, airy, a little corrupt. Fucking folk princess! It is a strait-jacket, this role, so she will hit back at the straitjacket, and everyone else who's helped to lock her in its sleeves: manager, record company executive, music store executive, rabid fan. But she will attack with style and an attention to craft. There won't be a single sound out of place, every last note exactly as she wants it. She will take back the murder, she will take back herself. Not that anyone else will care about that. Thirty-one years after the song's release, no one's even posted it on YouTube or Soundcloud. It is consigned to the forgotten. The audience proceeds as if Joni Mitchell is the writer of vulnerable songs that make us ache a little and sigh and wipe our eyes into our shirt cuffs.

This is a piece that wants to acknowledge and respect darkness. This piece is darker than some of my work, but Joni's song is a dark song, and I've always loved it for that. I wanted to write about why Joni might have wanted and needed to write such a thing. It is not a representative song, but I think it is one of her most beautiful songs.

WEREWOLVES OF LOS ANGELES

SEAN MURPHY

I've spent much time in recent weeks listening to, and at times wrestling with, Joni Mitchell's challenging, idiosyncratic and, one must finally say, brilliant album, Mingus, named after jazz great Charles Mingus, who wrote the music for four of the six compositions. When two one-of-a-kind artists collaborate to create a one-of-a-kind album, who should expect the results to be predictable? Still, the standout cut for me on the album is the least predictable of all. "The Wolf that Lives in Lindsey" is one of only two songs on the album that Mitchell wrote without collaboration from Mingus. It's not only the most unusual and least overtly jazzy number on the album, it's one of the most peculiar songs in her entire catalogue.

Is it jazz? It's certainly improvised, described by Mitchell as a duet between herself and the drummer Don Alias—with a background chorus provided by a pack of wolves. Mitchell's thrashing, growling acoustic guitar alternately slaps out drones from slackened strings, then scrapes harmonics from up the neck. Mitchell's voice soars, howls and harmonizes with the wolf-song, sometimes blending to the point where we're not sure which is human and which is beast—which is, of course, the point of the song. All of it is drenched in an eerie, atmospheric reverb that more than adequately summons the hollow menace of a star-filled, cold and dangerous night. Said Mitchell of the song: "I included it because the wolves constituted [Mingus'] musical concept about cacophony. Someone found me an actual tape to use, of wolves singing away, and it's beyond dissonance—it transcends dissonance."

Dissonance? Definitely; both in the music and the subject matter. And Mitchell is not just crying wolf: this stuff is dark. Who is this Lindsey? A pimp? Drug dealer? Addict? Rapist? Mass murderer? A stand-in for the darkness in all of us? Is he based on a real character, someone Mitchell knew? Is the Hollywood connection incidental, or might this character be an escapee from an old black and white horror flick? All of the above?

A song ought to stand on its own merits, without reference to outside sources. But I was intrigued enough by our anti-hero's unusual, androgynous name to dig around in some old interviews with Mitchell to see if I could find any clues. Big Bad Lindsey neither meets our usual lyrical preconceptions nor quite matches the name of a criminal who "loved the ways of darkness / Beyond belief." But, although Mitchell talks about the song in several interviews, she never provides a direct clue.

So we're on our own, which after all is where listeners would have found themselves in pre-internet 1979 when the album came out. Whether or not there's a real Lindsey somewhere out there, the song is clearly a take on the old werewolf legend, updated to a contemporary setting—"there lives a wolf in Lindsey that raids and runs through the hills of Hollywood and the downtown slums." Our lycanthropic Lindsey is able to "[get] away with murder" because far from firing silver bullets, the police are too distracted to pay attention to the "derelicts or ladies of the night" who are his apparent victims... or friends? Or perhaps even customers? For there's this rather inexplicable business of the "heavy heavy snow" there in the Hollywood hills, where snow almost never falls. If we take it literally, this is either an apocalypse that swirls in on the Sun Belt sin city—or, more metaphorically, a drug-laden white powder fuel for that "darkness in men's minds."

The darkness isn't entirely unrelieved though. Mitchell hints that the evil Lindsey will get his comeuppance:

> If you're smart or rich or lucky
> Maybe you'll beat the laws of man
> But the inner laws of spirit
> And the outer laws of nature
> No man can

We can only hope. But let's leave the final word to Joni Mitchell: "It's a strange piece of music… When the thing was over, we figured that magic had, in fact, occurred. As raw as it was, and as technically peculiar as it was, you couldn't beat it for spirit."

CHINESE CAFÉ/UNCHAINED MELODY

Caught in the middle—Carol
We're middle class
We're middle aged
We were wild in the old days
Birth of rock 'n' roll days
Now your kids are coming up straight
And my child's a stranger
I bore her
But I could not raise her
Nothing lasts for long
Nothing lasts for long
Nothing lasts for long
Down at the Chinese Café
We'd be dreaming on our dimes
We'd be playing
"Oh my love, my darling"
One more time

Uranium money
Is booming in the old home town now
It's putting up sleek concrete
They're tearing the old landmarks down now
They're paving over brave little parks—
Ripping off Indian land again
How long
How long
Short sighted business men
Ah—nothing lasts for long
Nothing lasts for long
Nothing lasts for long
Down at the Chinese Café
We'd be dreaming on our dimes
We'd be playing
"You give your love, so sweetly"
One more time

Christmas is sparkling
Out on Carol's lawn
This girl of my childhood games
Has kids
Nearly grown and gone
Grown so fast
Like the turn of a page
We look like our mothers did now
When we were those kids' age
Nothing lasts for long
Nothing lasts for long
Nothing lasts for long

Down at the Chinese Café
We'd be dreaming on our dimes
We'd be playing
"Oh my love, my darling
I've hungered for your touch
A long lonely time
And time goes by so slowly
And time can do so much
Are you still mine?
I need your love
I need your love
God speed your love to me"
(Time goes—where does the time go
I wonder where the time goes)

A THREAD OF JONI

JILL BULLOCK McALLISTER

A year ago, thanks to Facebook, I experienced my own "Chinese Café/Unchained Melody" moment. I was reunited, through a friend of a friend of a friend, with someone from my childhood. We had been the best of giggling girlfriends as soon as we met in fourth grade, and we continued our friendship through high school while facing the challenges of our teenage years. After graduation, our apparent connection went dark, disappeared, and a long time ago I had dismissed the notion of ever reconnecting with her.

Our time in high school was in the mid '70s. Lisa and I were finding a world that we were both craving. Lawrence Ferlinghetti, Emily Dickenson, Bob Dylan, Gary Snyder, Henry David Thoreau—whenever either of us came across a poet, writer, or musician for the first time, we weren't complete until we had shared it with the other. These thinkers and artists became our guides as we tried to uncover our own true thoughts and creativity. So of course our discovery of, and need for, Joni Mitchell and her poetry was inevitable.

Sometimes true friendships allow for deep understanding even when words aren't available. Lisa and I had more than our fair share of teenage weights, as we are now discovering about each other. Yet back then it seems we rarely wanted to waste our time together dwelling on them. There was such an exciting world that our muses were sharing with us, and listening to them allowed us to transcend our personal sadness.

At the same time, our young world views were being shaped by these mentors. And our own budding poetry was being stirred.

Joni especially taught us that love is about so much more than a simple fantasy, and gave us the promise of the depths to which future love would take us. She gave us the courage to look beyond our small, immediate world and pre-defined futures. She raised our awareness of social justice and personal freedoms. As Joni sang her stories, we internalized her words, reshaped our self-images, respected our own wildness and dreamed of all the places we might also see some day.

Now, thirty-seven years later, I find that the thread of Joni Mitchell that was sewn into both of our fabrics never unraveled from either of us. "Chinese Café" is not a regret for the days gone by, and not a lament that nothing lasts for long. The act of singing her youthful song from the past within the song of the present heals the regrets and the lamenting. That unchained melody is both a sweet memory and a present-day offering, just like my rediscovered friendship.

Joni Mitchell's influence has had a ripple effect that carries on in so many poets and artists today. Her creativity continues to find new homes that welcome her as Lisa and I originally did. Once upon a time, we too were at that Chinese Café, probably eating French fries, and we go back there now as often as we can. Our fabrics still share the same thread of Joni, coaxing us to reminisce, stirring our inner poets and inspiring us to continue to explore the present together. Thank goodness for that unchained melody, that unchained voice, that unchained spirit that was woven into our own spirits so many years ago. And thank goodness that she continues to create for all of us today.

CHINESE CAFÉ/UNCHAINED MELODY

LARRY KLEIN

"Nothing lasts for long." Truer words have never been written. There have been very few times in my life when I came in to play or work on a song and the song created the emotional reaction that "Chinese Café/Unchained Melody" did when I first heard it.

I think that we all have a few relatively basic existential dilemmas that haunt us throughout our lives and that, if we are engaged in a creative pursuit, we repeatedly try to articulate, focus and re-frame this dilemma from numerous perspectives throughout our lives. If you peel away all of the specifics, one can often find a single, irrevocable sorrow that is the source from which everything that you make, write or paint emanates. "Nothing lasts for long" is a knife that cuts through to that place for me.

After working together and becoming friends during the recording of the album *Wild Things Run Fast*, Joni and I went on to be married to each other for ten years and have continued to work together, even since we separated and divorced. Our life together in itself has felt like a lifetime to me. We drove across Canada together, and I saw all of the landmarks and imagery that informed her early life and that recur throughout this song and much of her work as a writer.

Many of us go through our entire lives attached to the notion that there are certain givens in our lives—certain pillars of stability that are absolutes that we can ground ourselves with and tie ourselves to. Like the archetypical image of the ship captain in a storm, we feel bound and tied to this wheel and to the notion that it will give us some kind of safety in the face of the impermanence of our world, the inevitably tragic quality of life and what has been called "absurdity" by the existentialist writer Albert Camus. One of the many gifts that Joni gave to me during our years together is the recognition of the fact that there are really no givens in life; any idea that we cling to must be continuously re-examined and must evolve throughout our life if it is not to become a simple blindfold or crutch that we can lean on. The only real stability upon which we can rely is the fact that there is no real stability or static permanence in life. It is a harsh lens through which to view life, and one that it is pretty much impossible to retreat from once you begin the journey towards this uncompromising and unattached point of view. Perhaps the circumstances that surround the early part of one's life, and the events that follow, dictate when, if ever, a person comes to have this uncompromising view of life. Prior to having this epiphany, which was one of a great many gifts that I received through our time together, my experience of life had a shallow and guarded quality that I can best describe as an "as if" kind of feeling—a feeling of being at once removed from both the joy and sorrow of life. I paid dearly for this sea change with years of being caught in the riptide of this realization, as I believe that Joni did at the time that she came to it, but I wouldn't trade it for anything.

There is a crisscrossing back and forth through a life that occurs in the lyric of "Chinese Cafe," from the present day realization that "we look like our mothers did now, when we were those kids' age," back to the joyful image of "dreaming on our dimes"; dancing to the jukebox as a teenager, but always landing between these chronological dissolves on the line "nothing lasts for long." She only lands on these images for long enough to establish the poignancy of the dilemma, then springs on to the next image of the thought. She somehow presents the images as one would think of them, without the distance of a specific, linear narrative. When I hear the poem, it feels like I am thinking it. Suffice to say that it is extremely rare to find this kind of writing in poetry, fiction or songwriting. Joni is often able to get there, throughout her body of work, and she certainly does in this song.

When I listen to the song now, it still hits me in my heart as strongly as it did the first time that I heard her play it in the studio. I see the wheat fields, the silos, the trains roaring across the prairie, the house that she grew up in, the school that she went to as a child. It propels me back into my own childhood, but from a vantage point from which I'm not afraid to feel the sorrow of impermanence. I see her mom and dad, and feel the strength of character that people had to have in order to build a life in the 1930s. I see the relative affluence and comfort of the time that we live through now, and the slack-jawed ambivalence that is one of its results. I see and feel the tragic aspect of scientific progress and the destruction of ancient beauty, as well as the transient quality of physical beauty and the pure and innocent joys of youth.

Once, during the time that Joni and I were married, I was driving back from the Southern California desert alone. I took a detour off of the highway near the Los Angeles suburb that I grew up in. It was the late evening, and I drove to the park near our house that I went to as a child. The owners who bought the house from my parents had eradicated every bit of beauty that I remembered our suburban front and back yard having. Concrete surrounded the small tract house, each of the old trees in our yard having long ago been cut down and pulled out of the ground. I got out of the car, walked into the center of the park and just stood there for about fifteen minutes, listening to the sounds of night, smelling the grass that grows in that park—a park that is utterly unremarkable aside from the fact that I spent so much of what felt like a relatively solitary childhood there. My early life raced by me in those minutes: lying on my back during afternoons, watching cloud formations cross the sky. Joys, sorrow, sadness, loneliness, sweet solitude; it all came surging through me. This song has that same effect on me every time I hear it, the flood of emotional memories rushing through me like those that ran through my mind, standing alone in that park at midnight, during a summer night.

LAKOTA

I am Lakota!
Lakota!
Looking at money man
Diggin' the deadly quotas
Out of balance
Out of hand
We want the land!
Lay down the reeking ore!
Don't you hear the shrieking in the trees?
Everywhere you touch the earth—she's sore
Every time you skin her—all things weep
Your money mocks us
Restitution—what good can it do?
Kennelled in metered boxes
Red dogs in debt to you

I am Lakota!
Lakota!
We're fighting among ourselves
All we can say with one whole heart
Is we won't sell
No we'll never sell
We want the land!
The lonely coyote calls
In the woodlands—footprints of the deer
In the barrooms—poor drunk bastard falls
In the courtrooms—deaf ears—sixty years
You think we're sleeping
But quietly
Like rattlesnakes and stars
We have seen the trampled rainbows
In the smoke of cars

I am Lakota
Brave
Sun pity me
I am Lakota
Broken
Moon pity me
I am Lakota
Grave
Shadows stretching
Lakota
Oh pity me

I am Lakota
Weak
Grass pity me
I am Lakota
Faithful
Rocks pity me
I am Lakota
Meek
Standing water
Lakota
Oh pity me

I am Lakota!
Lakota!
Standing on sacred land
We never sold these Black Hills
To the missile-heads—
To the power plants
We want the land!
The bullet and the fence—broke Lakota
The black coats and the booze—broke Lakota
Courts that circumvent—choke Lakota
Nothing left to lose

Tell me grandfather
You spoke the fur and feather tongues—
Do you hear the whimpering waters
When the tractors come?

Sun pity me
Mother earth
Mother
Moon pity me
Father sky
Father
Shadows
Stretching on the forest floor
Mother earth
Oh pity me

Grass pity me
Mother earth
Mother
Rocks pity me
Father sky
Father
Water
Standing in a wakan manner
Mother earth
Oh pity me

THIS AINT NO KUMBAYAH!

JAMISON MAHTO

"He was completely dedicated to his adopted culture; he maintained his fictional roots faithfully throughout his life and denied all rumors that he was not an American Indian. Hollywood's Indian community honored Cody for his longstanding contribution to native causes. Although he was not Cherokee, they acknowledged that his charitable deeds were more important than his heritage."

—*IOLA* on Iron Eyes Cody

I'm not Lakota.

Because being Lakota

Is a dream that

Just doesn't happen anymore

That all ended when the matron

Shoved the bar of soap down my throat

When she caught me speaking my own language.

From there I learned English.

I am Lakota

I'm the poor drunken bastard

Your Mama warned you about

Dancing with desperate dignity

in the rain at the corner

of 6th and Hennepin

lost in a nightmare

surrounded by false prophets

gonefishin' for seagulls on sandy beaches

where time doesn't rhyme with eternity

I am Lakota

doing a dance of defiance

in the face of your fear

I am of the same blood

as my brothers crazy horse and sitting bull

poet/warriors
prepared to take a bullet
for the people
I am Lakota
not Sicilian and raised on robbery
my jewelry is not made in Pakistan
and I don't speak French.

I am Lakota
my Sun Dance scars are self-inflicted
I am Lakota but no more than any other.
I am no more Lakota than Jackson Pollock
When he paints sweet grass camouflage in swirling blood dribbles
On the canvas exterior of the summer lodge.
I am no more Lakota than Marilyn Monroe
When she drives her sexuality into a pill bottle
Dream romance dripping with sweaty eroticism.
I am no more Lakota than my father
When he bails out of a B-25 Mitchell bomber
Over Sicily and North Africa as now
In a haze of cigar smoke, whiskey and factory hue
He don't speak of it much.
It ain't easy bein' Lakota
But I suppose if somebody's gotta be it,
I'm all right with it bein' me!

I am indigenous to this continent
I am the keeper of the flame
I am the steward of this land
I am the blood stained church floor
At the takeover of Wounded Knee
Yes, I am a card carrying member
Of the alliance of friends.

Yeah, the FBI, CIA, National Guard
And Goon Squads all fired on that church.
We lost some great warriors there
And we learned how to fight Giants there
And We learned to dream again, there.

We are all free to be who we want to be

If you understand that you understand much.
If you believe yourself to be Indigenous
and the community recognizes you to be such.
if you take your shirt off,
and I see Sundance piercings on your chest
That says the same thing to me as adopting an orphan.

There is something deeper
Than feathers and chants,
Sweat lodge, language and Sun Dance
it's far more important to be a man,
To be a member of the human race
And recognize that we all bleed red
We all put our pants on one leg at a time.
It's far more important that Iron Eyes Cody
married a native woman
And adopted two native children.
I've got a daughter that
I only just recently began to get to know
So, you see, things have changed.
I will see to it my daughter
That there are many safe bike trails
For you to ride in your future....

I am Lakota

I am Lakota

I am Lakota

I am Mahto Wakan
Spirit Bear

The Black Hills are not for sale
neither is this soul.
And this ain't no Kumbayah, baby!
Just so we understand each other.

Sometimes things happen for a reason, a reason that I don't understand.

My first encounters with Joni's music were in dimly lit, bohemian rooms full of interesting and suspicious aromas in a group of what were hippies sharing a couple of quarts of Ripple Wine. I noticed and appreciated the flow of the lyrics, and understood the ideas and sentiments contained in the words.

I was introduced to the piece "Lakota" on the *Chalkmark in a Rainstorm* album and was struck by the spare, blunt honesty of the lyrics, not to mention the chant intro performed by Iron Eyes Cody. This raised the issue of cultural misappropriation, since Iron Eyes Cody was Sicilian. I was angered by this. In order to understand my own anger, I pursued the issue further to find out that he married a Native woman and adopted two Native children. The Cherokee Tribe formally recognized his contributions to the community. It made me appreciate and understand more fully the human being and the man.

In the Native community, it is hard to gain acceptance but not unusual or uncommon. As my friend, the Irish Poet T.K. O'Rourke, once said, "I had to eat a lot of fry bread to get this far."

In a body of work that includes many high points over the span of a career, *Shadows and Light* stands as important to the music community and its audience as any of the great albums in history. It is brilliant when you surround yourself with the greats. I wish I could hang around with the likes of Weather Report.

How synchronous, then, that Mr. Cody after Ms. Mitchell led me to confront my own biases and prejudices regarding the importance of an ethnic background. While we know it is vitally important, there is something that transcends. Whether or not Joni was conscious of any of this isn't what matters. What matters is that the magic of art/music compels me to ask those questions.

Sometimes things happen for a reason that I don't understand. How magical is that?

CHEROKEE LOUISE

Cherokee Louise is hiding in this tunnel
In the Broadway bridge
We're crawling on our knees
We've got flashlights and batteries
We've got cold cuts from the fridge
Last year about this time
We used to climb up in the branches
Just to sway there in some breeze
Now the cops on the street
They want Cherokee Louise

People like to talk
Tongues are waggin' over fences
Waggin' over phones
All their doors are locked
God!
She can't even come to our house
But I know where she'll go
To the place where you can stand
And press your hands like it was bubblebath
In dust piled high as me
Down under the street
My friend
Poor Cherokee Louise

Ever since we turned thirteen
It's like a minefield
Walking to the door
Going out you get the third degree
And comin' in you get the third world war

Tuesday after school
We put our pennies on the rails
And when the train went by
We were jumpin' round like fools
Goin' "Look no heads or tails"
Goin' "Look my lucky prize"
She runs home to her foster dad
He opens up his zipper
And he yanks her to her knees
Oh please be here please
My friend
Poor Cherokee Louise

Cherokee Louise is hiding in this tunnel
In the Broadway bridge
We're crawling on our knees
We've got Archie and Silver Screen
I know where she is
She's in the place where you can stand
And press your hand like it was bubblebath
In dust piled high as me
Down under the street
My friend
Poor Cherokee Louise
Oh Cherokee Louise
Cherokee Louise

CREE MARY IS MY REAL NAME

BETH CUTHAND

Cree Mary is my real name not Cherokee Louise.
I know the mystery of the sea of green, the endless sky and more.
I gather the sweetgrass and the roots and braid them with my hands.
I've been washed clean by the river.
Oh, washed clean by the river.

I was the broken woman livin' under Broadway Bridge.
I knew the invasion of men's hands that ripped my soul away.
I felt the snow come creepin' in,
under my blanket of dust
drying my heart into a stone too hard to break or rust.

The little people whispered all cozy in their dens
dug deep into the river side beside my cold dark head.
They whispered to me slyly
trying to lure me to the deep of the river
icy river, that called me in my sleep.

Oh they whispered to me slyly trying to lure me to the deep.

Lying under Broadway Bridge I hid myself away
I wanted to give up and never walk away, just
crawl out on the ice and sleep the night away.

Cree Mary is my real name not Cherokee Louise.
I'm living and I'm loving. I'm sweet alive today.
cause I fed the little people some jellybeans and such.
I believed what people told me that they'd heal me if did.
I gave them candies oh sweet candies, made friends with them
And then

One fine spring dawn they lead me to the river,

Washed me clean

Oh, washed me in the water and the hands that hurt me

melted into the river's rush.

And somewhere in the wind a bright light danced down my open mouth.

I found my soul again that day

By believing oh believing that good could come my way.

Washed clean by the river, I live in this town today.

The university, the bridges, the Wanuskewin park,

They are mine. I earned them under the Broadway Bridge.

Oh I'm Cree Mary now Not Cherokee Louise.

I teach my grandchildren to feed the little people,

Respect the river and sing

Thanks to the grace of water

and the little people to wash the shadows clean.

It was 1969 when our family moved to Saskatoon as part of an "Urban Indian Relocation Program" devised by the Federal Department of Indian Affairs and Northern Development. It was an exciting time for me, as I transferred to the University of Saskatchewan and discovered the forbidden fruits of the big city.

Here I was in Joni Mitchell's home town. Rumors of her whereabouts were everywhere.

Joni was ours. She belonged to us. We were proud that a Saskatoon hometown girl was making it big. I think I eventually wore out three LPs of *Both Sides Now*.

I was a budding poet, if only in my own private mind, and she was the real thing. Like the bards of old, she sings the stories of our human existence with power and grace. Joni Mitchell is a bard for the twenty-first century as she was in the twentieth. The fusion of voice, word, music brings the story to life again and again.

While "Cherokee Louise" is gritty and sorrowful, and the Broadway Bridge still shelters the homeless, I asked myself: where is this woman today and what does she want to say?

The question bubbled around in my mind for months until she told me. I think my poem is a song, too; a song of a woman who lived beyond mere survival to take back her own name and face the memories that scared her but didn't hold her captive.

Today it is estimated that seventy percent of Native women in Canada are victims of male violence. It is to my sisters that I dedicate this poem. Thank you Joni Mitchell for your unwavering belief in the justice we seek and the grace we carry even so.

ABOUT TWO GIRLS

PATRICIA WILSON

Joni Mitchell's career, especially in music, has been long and varied; several platinum albums, but not one top ten hit. Still, for fans of her music, "girls like me," Joni Mitchell was almost a religion. I could identify with so very, very many of her songs, as though she were speaking directly to me. She was the one confidant that I could trust who was my age. She knew me through and through. The strum of her guitar, the sounds of her voice—a musical instrument in itself—the words to her songs: they told me she knew my angst, my troubles, my hope, my anger because they were hers too.

Many may believe that Joni Mitchell's music is no longer relevant in this society, if it ever really was. I disagree on both counts. To many of the younger generation, rap or hip hop is the music of relevance today because it tells the human story. Joni Mitchell's music always told her story, which was the human story as well, just in a different cadence. "Cherokee Louise" was, and still is, one of Joni Mitchell's lesser-known songs, but it shall ever remain one of my favorites.

From the first time I heard it, the music, and especially the words, to "Cherokee Louise" grabbed my heart and consciousness. I vividly remember placing my hand to my forehead, my heart beating a little faster. I was back to being a child—"that child of the '50s" who was never quite good enough no matter how many times I went to confession and mass; always suspect... up to no good certainly. I was guilty as charged, though at first I was too young to recognize my crime. It was only later, when I'd reached puberty, that I came to know the name of my crime: it was being female, a sinner of the worst sort, a Jezebel in the making.

Thirty-four years later, 1991, listening to Joni's album *Night Ride Home*, I heard "Cherokee Louise" for the first time. It brought back to me the wonderfulness of having a secret place to hide and read *Archie*, *Silver Screen* and the absolutely forbidden *True Romance* with my best girlfriend, Diane; shiny remembrances of make believe, games of tag and red rover, climbing trees, playing "Cowboys and Indians" just like the boys—of being "just kids" together. She and I were tarnished by "tongues waggin' over fences," thirteen being exactly what Joni Mitchell described: a "minefield / Walking to the door / Going out you get the third degree / And comin' in you get the third world war." Joni knew exactly how it had been. She'd been there right beside us, but I didn't know it then.

"Cherokee Louise" is about child sexual abuse, but it's also about the emotional abuse visited upon young girls of that era: one foot in the world of childhood, one toe into adulthood, pushed over the line too soon by the very adults who believed they were protecting us "for our own good." Fortunately for me, I never suffered any physical or sexual abuse. I don't know that any of my friends were victims of sexual abuse, but so many of them very definitely suffered physical abuse. Many of us were definitely subjected to the emotional abuse of some of our teachers, and within our churches, and sometimes even by our own parents just because we were "girls like us."

Even today, when I listen to "Cherokee Louise" I have visceral responses to it. Like Joni Mitchell, I'd always loved music and art. The words and music of "Cherokee Louise" conjure an image for me where I'm both Cherokee Louise and her unnamed friend (Joni Anderson?), as if I'm flying above looking down from the night sky, but also looking up from the tunnel under the Broadway Bridge for some saving grace—for rescue for the both of us. I see a blue-black night sky, stars that are pinpoints of light, silver glitter blown upward from the hands of two young girls as a prayer for love and safety.

CHEROKEE LOUISE

JOHN C. SANDERS

I bought my very first used Joni Mitchell record, *The Hissing of Summer Lawns*, in 1986, in L.A. I was a somewhat lost gay kid, looking for some meaning and inspiration, just sixteen years old. I had heard her on the radio often enough, but what drew me in was discovering, from reading the jacket of a Buffy Saint Marie album I had bought for ninety-nine cents, that she had written "The Circle Game." From there I began a love affair with all things Joni.

When Joni released *Night Ride Home* in 1991, I was a fledgling painter and poet in art school. I fell in love all over again. I practically lived in my art studio, steeped in Joni's poetry of songs. Her song "Cherokee Louise" is very close to my heart. When I first listened to the song, I had to turn back and replay it over and over again. I was in such a state of shock. The song opened a floodgate of emotion and brought back the memory of a rare touchstone meeting I had with a young Native American girl who by all accounts could have been Cherokee Louise.

When I was seven years old my mother and I lived in a large house on the border of a forest out in Michigan. One afternoon I had been eagerly exploring the woods when I came across a shelter. Inside were many of the older neighborhood kids and a young Native American girl who I had never seen before. The others made me promise not to tell any adults about her. Together they had successfully kept her "safe" for over two weeks. Her name was Cherolynne, she was fourteen years old and she had been hiding out in the woods in the shelter she had made for herself with the help of the other children. Soon enough I was contracted to return home to smuggle food from my mother's kitchen; I went home and stole hot dogs, cold cuts, bread and cookies. My mother must have noticed me dragging my haul across the lawn, and she followed me out into the woods. This is how Cherolynne came to live in our house. My mother intervened and offered Cherolynne a room of her own in our big, empty house. Cherolynne's story was soon revealed: you see she had run away from the reservation because her stepfather had been sexually molesting her.

Cherolynne lived with my mother and me for the rest of that summer and through the holiday season. Her presence did not go over well with many of our neighbors. There was a lot of gossip and disapproval being expressed over Cherolynne's presence and her popularity amongst the local kids. However ridiculous people can be, we still managed to have a great time. I remember running around the neighborhoods and out into the woods with Cherolynne and the other children. It's possible to find love with an incredible sense of freedom and mystery even in the presence of the darkest shadows. In the midst of tragedy flowed poetry in motion—the fullness of life being lived. Eventually Cherolynne moved back to the reservation, and I never saw her again. When I listen to Joni's song, it literally hits home. I have always been deeply moved by Joni's poetry and songs, and those friends that share my appreciation share a significant bond. A tale like "Cherokee Louise" touches upon deep threads in our overall culture; so many children are sexually abused, and for those of us who have endured sexual abuse, having it mirrored back with such compassion can be incredibly healing. What strikes me most is Joni's use of the truth. There is a fearless honesty in Joni's writing and voice that inspires me to risk expressing my own personal truth. As an artist I have been inspired and challenged by Joni's honesty. To make art with truth is a powerful act and Joni makes art with a capital "T."

"Cherokee Louise" brought with it the memory of Cherolynne and my own lost childhood. I had pushed them far back, along with the memory of my own abuse. As I began to recall my past experiences, I was washed in waves of grief. I just cried and cried over everything: I cried for Cherolynne, I cried for Cherokee Louise and I cried for my own lost truth. I can honestly say that Joni's work has this kind of import, and I am eternally grateful. Now my art is stronger, more open, more honest and I'm writing again—poetry, stories and now even a few songs.

Thank you, Joni.

SEX KILLS

I pulled up behind a Cadillac
We were waiting for the light
And I took a look at his license plate
It said "JUST ICE"
Is justice just ice?
Governed by greed and lust?
Just the strong doing what they can
And the weak suffering what they must?
And the gas leaks
And the oil spills
And sex sells everything
And sex kills
Sex kills

Doctors' pills give you brand new ills
And the bills bury you like an avalanche
And lawyers haven't been this popular
Since Robespierre slaughtered half of France!
And Indian chiefs with their old beliefs know
The balance is undone—crazy ions—
You can feel it out in traffic
Everyone hates everyone!
And the gas leaks
And the oil spills
And sex sells everything
And sex kills
Sex kills

All these jackoffs at the office
The rapist in the pool
Oh and the tragedies in the nurseries
Little kids packin' guns to school

The ulcerated ozone
These tumors of the skin
This hostile sun beating down
On this massive mess we're in!
And the gas leaks
And the oil spills
And sex sells everything
And sex kills
Sex kills
Sex kills
Sex kills
Sex kills

TIDES

PETER KOUZMOV

It is Sofia, Bulgaria, the '80s. I am in a Soviet-style building, musicians and artists crammed in a studio on the 12th floor. We only have money for cheap cigarettes and alcohol. Outside, Communism and Chernobyl surround us.

Every 4 am your voice fills the air as are waiting for the sun. Joni—my piano teacher says through a cloud of cigarette smoke. We don't understand a word of English. The voice, your voice, sometimes urgent, sometimes soft, with its high and low tides carries us off into our dreams at 5 am.

It is the '90s. The Berlin Wall is gone and I live in the City of Angels. 100 degrees and I am clutching a copy of *Turbulent Indigo*. "Sex kills..." you sing. In the next room Bill is dying of AIDS. The avalanche of bills spilling on the floor, the factory of scattered pills on the table, the gang down the street by the Greyhound station playing with car alarms and guns, friends committing suicide.

It is San Francisco, and everyone speaks of Y2K. I am sitting in a Kaiser Permanente workshop—"Simple Tools for Battling Depression." I so badly want depression to be simple. In walks Randy, who says, "Listen to Joni," and asks me if I am in the sex trade. Suddenly I remember your voice, and he and I become soul mates forever.

It is the 21st Century and the Twin Towers are gone. I flee to Bulgaria because I want a hug. We listen to your songs. It is a new era, and we understand every word you say. We cannot imagine there ever was a time we did not. "Is justice just ice?" Joni, the oil spills have become Technicolor spectacular, and sex kills on a global scale—like the country you and I have adopted.

On the phone, I hear your voice in the background. Randy is creating a collage or a poem with you in it. And I say, "Randy, how many times can you listen to the same songs?" And he says, "What a question," exhaling smoke into the receiver. He asks me how life is in the Nation's Capital, and we guess what you would say about it.

Joni, we are here—at the crossing point where Bulgaria and Canada meet.
Your songs are the place where space and time intersect, their tides carry everything and everyone I have known. And I want to know more, and more, and more again.